House Fever

HOUSE

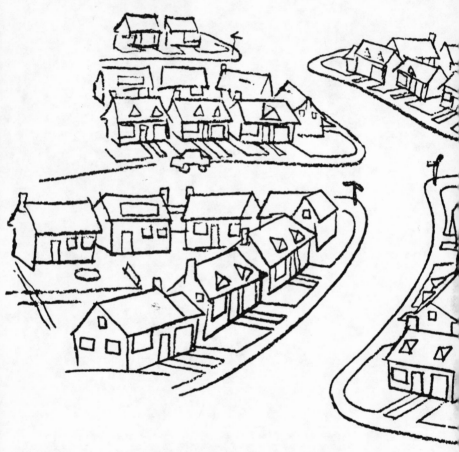

Illustrated by Rowland B. Wilson

and William C. Andrews

FEVER

The Money Crunch
Inflation Fighter's Guide
to Buying, Selling,
Remodeling, and Decorating
Your Home

by

Michael Braunstein

Harcourt Brace Jovanovich

New York and London

Requests for permission to make copies of
any part of the work should be mailed to:
Permissions, Harcourt Brace Jovanovich, Inc.
757 Third Avenue, New York, N.Y. 10017

Set in Linotype Fairfield and Electra Bold

Printed in the United States of America

Library of Congress Cataloging in Publication Data

Braunstein, Michael.
House fever.

1. House buying. 2. House selling.
3. Home ownership. I. Title.
HD1379.B73   643   79-2959
ISBN 0-15-142182-X

B C D E

Dedicated to Madame Tran Van Kha

Acknowledgments

Many of my friends, business associates, and relatives have been generous with their suggestions, unsparing criticisms, and inspirational ideas. I'll always remember what they did for me. The only ones whose names I can still recall, however, are: William Andrews, William Arthur, Dick Bibart, Carole Braunstein, Tom Brower, Fred Drenning, Brian Dumaine, Shep Ferguson, Vern Fowler, David Fox, John Helgerson, David Junka, James D. Klingbeil, Janet Lantz, Holmes Miller, Carl Novotny, Dan O'Reilly, Betty Lou Ruch, Ellen Ryan, Annette Trembly, and Rowland Wilson.

Special thanks to Carol Hill, Andrew Tobias, Ann Kochman, Larry Abramson, and my wife, Suzanne.

Contents

Hors d'Oeuvres

Birds do it. Bees do it. Even chimpanzees do it. But somehow *they* muddle by without monumental mortgage payments, escalating utility bills, and microwave ovens. This is the story of the nesting habits of twentieth-century Americans. If you think mating is tricky, wait till you try nesting.

There is a great similarity between the mating and nesting rituals. A fantastic home is capable of stirring souls with desire. Many couples want a new home with the same urgency as they want each other. The rising cost of homes often requires the earnings of a two-paycheck marriage. Two can't live as cheaply as one, but their combined borrowing power is greater.

The chapters to come may be a bit weak on barebreasted maidens, handsome young warriors, and fertility rites, but the pages abound with buying, selling, sweating, and fretting. Buyers and sellers alike bemoan the difficulties of high interest rates, uncertain economic times ahead, and increasing energy costs. But *House Fever,* spiced with anecdotes from my own and other people's fortunes and misfortunes, shows you how to make every real-estate deal a better deal.

I do not claim to be a dispassionate observer of the scene. Recently my wife, Suzanne, and I suffered from a debilitating case of "house fever." Writing this book is part of the therapy prescribed by my doctors, along with practicing yoga while humming "Home Sweet Home."

These days I can be found on the grounds of our newly acquired estate, muttering to myself about peeling paint, sod webworm, and unreliable repairmen. I am older, wiser, and deeper in debt than the starry-eyed romantic I once was. But I can't resist the urge to share the lessons I have learned. After all, as Oscar Wilde said, "The only thing to do with good advice is to pass it on."

Good-bye Rolling Stone, Hello Architectural Digest

Do you remember the time in your life when you put down *Jack & Jill* and picked up *Seventeen?* Or how about the day when you gave up *Boys' Life* for the pleasures of *Playboy?* Aging campus radicals are turning middle class and buying homes. Many have just discovered that a "stud" is a piece of wood holding up a house and not a cool dude. The current trend is to switch from *Rolling Stone* to *Architectural Digest*. I wouldn't be surprised if, to sustain its circulation, *Rolling Stone* begins to feature articles on "Growing Avocado Pits" and "Remodeling Your Kitchen."

House fever is often accompanied by a similar fever for new furnishings and decorations. I knew I had reached a crossroads in life when I picked up *Playboy* magazine the other day and turned to the centerfold. There she was, a seductive, barely clothed young maiden spread deliciously over a chair, and the first thing I noticed was the chair.

Housing Hall of Fame

Some men and women test the limits of their ingenuity and endurance as they climb to the summit of their chosen field. I would like to nominate to the Housing Hall of Fame a few such individuals whom we encountered during our bout with house fever:

Hy List

Hy List, real-estate agent *extraordinaire,* won his place in the Hall of Fame for valor under fire. When Hy first started on the job, his boss told him simply to bring "willing" buyers and "willing" sellers together. After twenty years in the business, Hy has yet to meet a "willing" buyer or seller. Almost all of his clients could more realistically be categorized as "frenzied," "unrealistic," "greedy," "difficult," "frightened," "uncertain," and sometimes downright "irrational."

After spending six weeks showing one couple every stark contemporary house in town, Hy did not let out so much as a whimper when they changed their minds and finally decided that a gingerbread Victorian might suit them better.

Hy never gave up when another couple asked him to find

a five-bedroom dream house complete with indoor pool for under $40,000, and he's still out there looking.

A year ago, Mr. List was able to persuade one seller to accept an offer of only $100,000 for his twenty-five-year-old converted garage which featured two rooms totaling 850 square feet, complete with half bath and a spacious quarter lot. A bit pricey, as the English say. Reluctantly, the man agreed to sell. Now, twelve months later, he still goes around muttering, "I should have held out for top dollar!"

Hy's efforts have brought success, not to mention a six-figure commission income. But some days it's hard to imagine what keeps him going. Whatever it is, Hy, we want you to have our best wishes as you drive off into the sunset in your new Mercedes 450 SEL.

Herman Hindsight III

Apartment dweller Herman Hindsight III won his place in the Housing Hall of Fame for his ten-year standing record of hesitating to buy a home because he felt that both the purchase price and the mortgage interest rate were always too high.

Herman first rejected a three-bedroom ranch house in Toledo priced at $27,000 in 1969. Subsequently regretting his hesitation, Herman narrowly missed purchasing the same home for $34,000 in 1972, when mortgage interest rates were 7½ percent. Hindsight shuddered and finally stopped himself at the last moment. This year Herman told us that he is seriously considering the identical house at a bargain price of $70,000 with mortgage financing

"At a single bound? . . . Are you kidding?!"

available at 12 percent interest. Herman says he is ready
to close the deal the minute the savings and loan associations agree to lower the mortgage rate to 8 percent. Fat
chance, Herman!

Herman is a descendant of a long line of procrastinators.
Great-Grandpappy Hindsight was going to be part of the
Oklahoma Sooners, but he never made it to the starting
line. Thereafter he was nicknamed "Herman the Later."
Herman's father almost bought a penthouse condominium
in San Diego during the early 1960s for $35,000. Having
hesitated to do so, he now spends his retirement years
at the Castle Court Mobile Home Park in Moline,
Illinois.

Murph the Turf

Murph is the owner of a large lawn-service company.
I discovered Murph by asking our neighbors to recommend someone to care for the lawn. One neighbor had
used Murph's services and suggested that I give him a call.

Murph the Turf looks a lot like Sam Snead and makes
almost as much money. He combines the charm of a
southern gentleman with the outdoor rugged good looks
of an aging duck hunter. He arrived in his pickup truck,
dressed in a plaid woolen jacket straight out of L. L. Bean's
catalog.

When I asked him to estimate the cost of taking care
of our lawn, he pulled out a printed four-page legal-size
form that listed all the categories of work he might perform. This covered everything from mowing to trimming,
picking up the clippings, mulching, weeding, applying
fertilizer, thatching, sodding, edging, pruning, seeding,

controlling broadleaf weeds, exterminating billbugs, water-
ing, and removing leaves. Murph had so many items on
his list that you could hear my grass sigh and moan at the
thought of all that attention.

For the cost of Murph's lawn care I could take my wife
and son on an around-the-world cruise or spend a few
months at a health spa getting myself in shape. He never
flinched as he described the long list of services our lawn
required and their cost.

Suzanne and I finally settled on what Murph called a
"basic" program, which costs only half as much as a trip
around the world. It would be cheaper to fly our lawn to
the Virgin Islands for a few weeks in the sun than to have
Murph the Turf come by. But what would the neighbors
say?

Jacques d'Accord

Jacques d'Accord is to Houston what Chippendale was
to London. Jacques specializes in designing and building
French period furniture "customized" to the whims of
Texas oil and cattle multimillionaires.

His clients like to talk Texas. Their attitude is "We're
rich as a bitch and look how folksy we are. We talk hogs
and hominy but enjoy caviar and Louis XVI antiques."

One client entered his studio and drawled, "Hiyah,
Jacques. My, this here little desk sure does look mighty
nice. I want you to make me one like it, only bigger. Add
a few more drawers big enough to hold some Bourbon,
and I don't mean the King."

When a matron insisted on furniture styled in the
period of the nonexistent Louis XVII, Jacques outdid him-

self. He designed for her some ornate nursery furniture, because the poor Crown Prince never attained puberty.

Another client confided that she was bored with all the Louis XV and XVI furniture. She wanted to take home some pieces made in the style popular during Napoleon's reign. Jacques looked at her with admiration. In his thick French accent he announced, "Madame, Empire is my bag!"

Jacques d'Accord is an imaginative craftsman with exquisite taste. He will go down in history as the man responsible for inventing the Empire-style hitching post, the Louis XVI swivel armchair, and the vibrating Louis XV chaise longue. Only recently a Texan grande dame asked Jacques to construct a guillotine that she could use as a food processor. Jacques replied, "One blade or two?"

Nimble Nick

Once upon a time in the Kingdom of Suburb, there lived a King who was very, very sad because his castle was in a state of great disrepair. He sent off all his mighty knights on a quest for someone who could repair his home. The King had the knights proclaim throughout the land that whosoever could help him would receive the lovely Princess Philomena as his bride.

The poor King spent days on the highest tower of the castle, straining his eyes in search of the returning knights. Sadly, though, the knights brought back many repairmen whose promises were always more enchanting than their deeds. The doors were still jammed; the floors still creaked and groaned.

One day a man rode by the castle on his horse. He

carried a small leather satchel and was playing a flute. The music charmed the King, whose spirits were sinking fast.

"Lower the drawbridge," cried the King. "Let that man enter with his flute. If no one can fix my castle, at least this man's music will bring joy to my heart."

Nimble Nick, for such was the name of the man with the flute, rode through the courtyard of the castle and was quickly admitted to the throne room. The King entered with his court and sat down on the throne. Unfortunately, as the King sat down the throne creaked and broke.

Seeing this, Nimble Nick rushed to help the King and exclaimed, "Your Majesty, let me fix that throne. No King who loves music as you do should have to put up with such rickety furniture."

No sooner said than done. Nimble Nick took out a few tools from his leather satchel and transformed the old chair into an enchanting new throne. Seeing how well the musical carpenter had fixed the throne, the King led him through the castle pointing out to him the various things that needed to be repaired.

Nimble Nick was the answer to the King's prayers. Once in a while Nick would put down his tools and pick up his flute, and melodious sounds filled the halls. Soon the castle was miraculously transformed by the hands of the musical, magical master carpenter.

The King announced to the whole kingdom that the castle was once again beautiful and that Nimble Nick had won the hand of Princess Philomena. Church bells pealed and flocks of white turtledoves were set free.

Prince Nick and his bride lived happily ever after in

the King's castle. The King was elated because he didn't lose a daughter but gained a carpenter.

Moral: *A man's home is his hassle.*

Help! I Can't Stop Reading the Ads Even After We've Bought the House

You can't get chicken pox twice, but that's not true about house fever. Do you new homeowners still wake up early on Sunday mornings in a cold sweat and run to the front door to see if the Sunday paper has arrived? Even after signing the purchase contract I couldn't break myself of the 6:00 A.M. dash for the Sunday ads habit.

Shortly after we moved into our new house, I met another family who had also just moved into the neighborhood. They were in the midst of redecorating their newly acquired home from the attic to the basement.

"I know this sounds crazy," the wife confided, "but we're still looking at houses. Last week a home that we've admired for a long time came on the market, and we went to see it. Luckily it was awful inside or I don't know what we'd have done."

"You must be insane!" I cried, as spasms of laughter shook my body. "You can't be serious. In the middle of redecorating, you are out looking again? You don't still read the Sunday ads, do you?"

"Three weeks ago there was a terrific house on Lincoln Street listed in the paper," she admitted. "We didn't

actually go to see it, but we couldn't resist calling to find out the price. They were asking $80,000 for it."

"You don't mean the white house on the corner?"

"Yes, that's the one," she said.

"Well, they must have decided to lower the price. In this week's Sunday paper it was listed for only $75,000," I blurted out.

"Aha!" she shouted. "You're still looking at the ads too!"

House Hunting

Joy of House Hunting

Hello, sports fans. Welcome to the wild world of house hunting. Football may be the country's leading spectator sport, but house hunting tops the participant sports in popularity. Americans cover more miles house hunting than playing tennis or jogging. For every couple donning tennis togs, a dozen others are out chasing the elusive dream house. If the Olympic Games ever include the "house hunting" event in the schedule, the United States should take gold, silver, and bronze medals every year.

House hunting is governed by a complex set of metaphysical relationships that serve as a foundation for understanding the universe. Here, for the first time, is an eye-opening series of revelations known as *Braunstein's Laws:*

Braunstein's First Law of House Hunting: The house you are looking for doesn't exist at a price you can afford.

Braunstein's Law of Probability: The odds are that no matter what type of house you initially have in mind, you'll end up with something different.

Braunstein's Profit Principle: Buy high, sell higher.

Braunstein's Law of Regret: If you think on closing day that you may be making a mistake, two months later you'll be sure.

My best advice for house-hunting inflation fighters is to be on the lookout for a home with solid gold faucets, brass doorknobs, copper plumbing, and a promising geological formation indicating possible oil and gas reserves beneath the back lawn. If you buy a house like this, you'll probably fare pretty well fighting inflation, even if the bottom falls out of the housing market.

WARNING! House hunting can be hazardous. When driving by a spectacular home, do you slow down to a near standstill? Are your eyes on the house or the road? Perhaps the neighbors have already spotted you casing the house. If you suspect that someone has already called the police to report your license number, you may be right.

It's just too embarrassing to stop and park in front of the house. Instead, try to catch a glance while passing by at a normal rate of speed. This procedure can easily be repeated by the continuous execution of right turns. Then you are circling the block, afraid to stop, yet too enchanted to go on.

Frankly, the anticipation may be more enjoyable than the actual experience of living there. So don't miss the chance to savor every waiting moment.

Sporting contests take their toll on the players. House hunting can likewise be a grueling experience that leaves you weary and confused. It's not uncommon to visit five or more houses in a single afternoon during the frantic search for *the* home.

Hal and Wanda Lust were exhausted. They had just finished house hunting and were driving home. Hal told Wanda that he wanted to buy the gray colonial house on the hill, the second of six houses they had visited that day.

"The thing I like best about the house," he explained, "is the guest bedroom with bath right over the garage. That's what really clinched it for me."

"But Hal, you've got it all wrong," Wanda corrected him. "The gray colonial doesn't have a guest bedroom over the garage. That was in the first house we looked at this afternoon, the pseudo-Tudor with a slate roof."

"Maybe you're right," he reluctantly agreed, "but I still like that gray colonial. Don't you love its big country kitchen?"

"Yes, I do, but the country kitchen wasn't in the gray colonial either. It was the only good feature we found in the cedar split-level at Euphoria Acres."

"Well, if that's the way you feel, Wanda, let's just forget it," he grumbled. "Now that I think about it, you're confused too. The guest room over the garage was actually in the brick traditional we looked at yesterday; I think . . ."

It's not a bad idea to take along a Polaroid camera and plenty of film during your next house-hunting expedition. You might also want a pad and a pencil to sketch the floor plans of the homes. Most real-estate agents have fact sheets that list pertinent details of the houses you'll visit. Don't get so excited that you forget to take these home with you.

Some families have been known to buy a house because of a terrific fireplace in the family room, only to discover after the closing that the fireplace was in the ranch down the street—or was it the center-hall colonial house two blocks away?

Sing a Song of Sixpence

Many potential home buyers are caught in a squeeze between the goal of home ownership as an inflation hedge and the money crunch of high mortgage interest rates.. When times get rough, people turn to music to express their troubles and woes. A friend of mine recently came back from a meeting with a mortgage loan officer and was humming the musical score from *Oklahoma,* that well-known American classic. With apologies to Richard Rodgers and Oscar Hammerstein II, my friend began to sing—

>   *Oh-for-a-Home-ah!*
>   (To be sung to the tune
>   of "Oklahoma")
>
>   Oh-for-a-Home-ah
>   Like the one my mom and papa got
>   With ten rooms so sweet
>   With plenty of heat
>   And a scenic inflation-hedging lot.
>
>   Oh-for-a-Home-ah
>   Where our kids can romp and play all day.
>   If the bank says yes
>   We'll do our best
>   To pay off the mortgage one fine day.

We want to belong to the land
But the cost of the land is too grand.

So when they say . . .
It's 12½ percent we'll have to pay . . .
They're only saying
You can't afford a new home-ah
Come and see us another day, OK?

Oh, What I'd Do with Some Money
(To be sung to the tune of
"Oh What a Beautiful Morning")

Oh, what I'd do with some money
Oh, what I'd do with some dough
I'd buy a beautiful tract house
With a large lawn to water and mow.

There's a pretty ranch house in Encino
And a spacious split level in the Valley
But the interest rates high
As an elephant's eye
And it looks like it's climbing
Right up to the sky.

Oh, what I'd do with some money
Oh, what I'd do with some dough
I'd buy a beautiful tract house
With a yard where some flowers could grow.

I can't afford the down payment
My savings balance is nil
The way the economy's going
I can't afford to sit still.

"Refrain"

Mommy and Daddy I love you
I'm your loyal son so true blue.
If you would provide a down payment
I could move out by age forty-two.

The Name Game

Real-estate developers have discovered that houses sell
faster when they are located on streets with romantic names
and in subdivisions whose names connote natural beauty
or financial opulence.

After bulldozing every tree in sight to level the land
for easy development, the builders then proceed to anoint
the scorched earth with the most elegant and prestigious
names that the human mind can conjure up.

In your search for a new house, don't be misled by the
name. You may be enchanted by the prospect of living
in a subdivision called Maple Hill Canyon Estates. A tour
through the charmingly decorated model home distracts
you from the reality that there are no maples, no hills, no
canyons, and no estates. You're not alone. I almost bought
a house on a street named "Teeway" that wasn't even on
a golf course. That was too much for me to bear.

What's in a name? Often, not much. The topography
of most places named Maple Hill Canyon Estates often
resembles the Bonneville Salt Flats. Alpine View usually
overlooks the parking lot of a shopping center. Ten Oaks

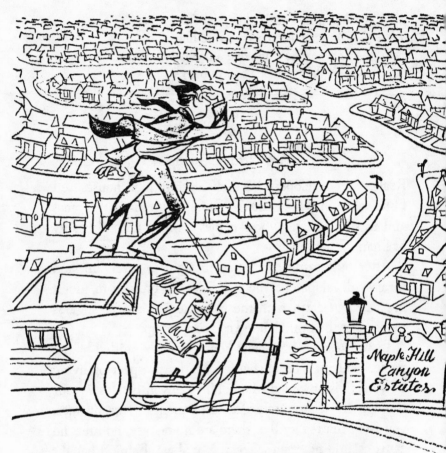

"Here's the ad. 'Unique opportunity! Deluxe custom executive model ideally situated in exclusive Maple Hill Canyon Estates. . . .'"

is lucky to have three pine trees. Harbor Knoll Village may be located in a cornfield, and Timber Brook is likely to have neither trees nor water. But who would buy a house at Platted Prairie?

The Three Biggest Pitfalls to Avoid

Most pitfalls are not obvious to the average house hunter. It takes a super sleuth to spot the clues, make the appropriate logical deductions, and sidestep the hazards. Because I have chosen to spotlight the three biggest pitfalls, it seems fitting to request the assistance of three world-famous detectives:

Jack Hammer and the Erector Set

Mona Pincher was standing in my office, her breasts swelling tautly against a cashmere sweater.

"I'd like you to help me," she said. "I signed a contract with the Ajax Construction Company to build my new house and they haven't completed a lot of things they were supposed to do. Ajax has taken my last dollar. I couldn't pay you for your services."

"They're going to have their hands full with you, sweetheart."

Mona's tongue wet her lips as she looked up, laughing. "Wouldn't *you* like to have your hands filled with me, Jack?"

I said I'd try to help her. I told her not to worry; we'd think of some way to work it out.

I got into a taxi and went over to Ajax corporate headquarters. The manager was a slimy little slob I couldn't stand.

"Does the name Mona Pincher mean anything to you?" I asked him.

"Yeah. She's the dame that drove us crazy with all those change orders for her house," he sneered.

"Well, she said that your company refused to come back to finish the job. She's stuck with four warped doors, unpainted trim molding, no gutters on two sides of the house, cracks in the drywall, and zero landscaping. I'm here to tell you that if these items aren't fixed by tomorrow night, the Ajax Construction Company will be *boom boom boom* right down the drain. You got that, punk?" I said, as the cold steel barrel of my .45 pressed against his gut.

The next day Ajax fixed everything on the list. Mona was very grateful. Her mouth was moist and open as she started lowering the straps of her slip. When she rushed into my arms, I could feel the surge of desire go through me.

"Next time, baby," I told her, "make sure you put some of the purchase money in a cash escrow account with a reliable third party to guarantee completion. That's your best protection," I murmured as I took her in my arms.

Traffic Most Foul

Miss Jane Murple was well acquainted with everyone in the village of St. Mead Mary. She was fluffy and dithery in appearance, but the seventy-year-old pink-cheeked Miss Murple was as shrewd as they come.

The time had arrived to consider leaving the village to buy a home in the city, where up-to-date hospitals and medical assistance would be close at hand. Her dear nephew, Raymond East, had taken the trouble to round up an estate agent who could show her various city homes. Miss Murple was fond of her nephew, but she rather doubted that she would enjoy leaving the tranquillity of St. Mead Mary.

A short visit to several fine residential areas seemed to suggest that the move might not present any problems. The very first afternoon of house hunting with Lance Fontana, the estate agent, turned up two or three good homes on quiet streets. Lance was a charming young man with a winning smile and great self-assurance. He confidently recommended the neighborhood. "Still," thought Miss Murple, "something tells me these homes are not as they should be."

That evening, while she was knitting, Miss Murple started to close her eyes as though falling asleep. Then she gave a gentle, ladylike little laugh. "Of course," she realized with incredible swiftness. "I prescribe a visit to those homes during the early morning rush hour."

As she told her nephew Raymond later, "I was right to suspect that the cars would be whizzing by in the early morning. The noise was deafening. I never really trusted that young Lance Fontana from the start. After all, I've known his kind before, even in my little village. So you see," she concluded, "it really turned out to be very simple. It was merely a case of traffic most foul."

The Adventures of Sherlock Homes

"My dear Watson," cried Sherlock Homes in uncontrolled astonishment, "surely you cannot seriously be considering this house?"

"Good heavens! I am most definitely interested in consummating the purchase at once. Is there any item to which you wish to call my attention?"

"To the curious incident of the storm windows in the study," said he.

"Why Homes, I do not recall there being any storm windows in the study," I protested.

"*That* was the curious incident," Homes remarked with a mischievous twinkle, as he continued to puff on his pipe.

"Well, what of it?"

"Did you notice," said Homes, "that today's newspaper lying in the entry hall just blew open to the sports section after the front door was closed? And what was the owner's explanation for the clear vinyl tacked to the outside of the bedroom windows?"

"My dear Homes, I hardly see where this is getting us. There is a strawberry pie in the fridge, too, but I don't see what any of this has to do with my purchasing this house."

"A little patience, Watson. Ask to see the utility bills for the past year. I think you will be amazed."

Watson returned a few moments later with a handful of old utility bills. He was visibly shaken and looked quite pale. "They're astoundingly high, as you suggested. But how did you know?"

"Elementary, my dear Watson," Sherlock Homes said

with his enigmatic smile, as he picked up his hat and turned to the door.

Looking for Clues— the Inspection Checklist

It's a big thrill to solve a tough whodunit. Outwitting the cunning criminal may be child's play next to the job of uncovering pitfalls while tracking down your dream house.

House-hunting enthusiasts usually can't make much use of a disguise kit, bloodhounds, or even a crime lab, but a home-inspection checklist might come in handy.

Make an eyewitness inspection at the scene of the crime. Then fill in the rating chart using the following point scale:

10 = Fantastic
 5 = Average
 1 = The Pits
 0 = Doesn't come with the house— you'll either have to buy it or do without it

Add up the ratings on the checklist. Take the sum of the ratings and divide it by the amount of money you *think* you'll have left in the bank after you make the down payment for the house and pay for redecorating and furniture. If the number you come up with is less than 1, either you deserve the Benjamin Franklin Thrift Award or you have grossly underestimated the cost of decorating and furnishing. If the number you arrive at is greater than 1, on behalf of most homeowners in America, "Welcome to the Club!"

HOME BUYER'S INSPECTION CHECKLIST

	Rating (0–10)	Comments
Exterior		
Garage size	_____	_____
Storm windows	_____	_____
Condition of paint	_____	_____
Condition of siding	_____	_____
Decorative lights	_____	_____
Driveway	_____	_____
Fences	_____	_____
Foundation	_____	_____
Chimney	_____	_____
Electric garage door opener	_____	_____
Gutters/downspouts	_____	_____
Pool	_____	_____
Tennis courts	_____	_____
Porch and patio space	_____	_____
Roof and shingles	_____	_____
Security lights	_____	_____
Shutters/awnings	_____	_____
Screens	_____	_____
Storage place for tools	_____	_____

	Rating (0–10)	Comments

Grounds and Landscaping

	Rating (0–10)	Comments
Children's play area	_____	_____
Playground equipment	_____	_____
Flowers	_____	_____
Fountains, operable	_____	_____
Greenhouse	_____	_____
Mature trees	_____	_____
Lawn	_____	_____
Lot drainage (away from house)	_____	_____
Lot size	_____	_____
Shrubs, condition and appearance	_____	_____
Sidewalks, condition	_____	_____
Site elevation	_____	_____
Space for garden plot	_____	_____
Watering system	_____	_____

Air Conditioning/Heating/Insulation

	Rating (0–10)	Comments
Balanced flow of air throughout house	_____	_____
Central air conditioning	_____	_____
Dehumidifier/ humidifier	_____	_____
Economical type fuel (1 for electric)	_____	_____
Electronic air filter	_____	_____

	Rating (0–10)	Comments
Energy efficient	_____	_____
Thermal windows	_____	_____
Heat pump	_____	_____
Heating/air-conditioning equipment size sufficient	_____	_____
Insulation	_____	_____
Registers, radiators, or baseboards adequate	_____	_____
Solar heating system	_____	_____
Condition of furnace	_____	_____
Weatherstripping and caulking	_____	_____

Basement or Crawl Space

	Rating	Comments
Adequate lighting	_____	_____
Dryness	_____	_____
Flooring	_____	_____
Free from musty odor	_____	_____
Remodeling possibilities	_____	_____
Structural elements sound	_____	_____
Termites	_____	_____
Sump pump	_____	_____
Waterproofing	_____	_____
Wall cracks	_____	_____

	Rating (0–10)	Comments

Kitchen

Cabinets and counter
space   _____   _____

Electrical outlets for
minor appliances   _____   _____

Floor covering   _____   _____

Kitchen arrangement   _____   _____

Lighting sufficient   _____   _____

Microwave oven   _____   _____

Pantry   _____   _____

Proximity to garage   _____   _____

Range   _____   _____

Vented range hood   _____   _____

Refrigerator/freezer   _____   _____

Window overlooking
play area   _____   _____

Bathrooms

Bathtub   _____   _____

Condition of fixtures   _____   _____

Conveniently located   _____   _____

Drawer and cabinet
space   _____   _____

Electrical outlets   _____   _____

Exhaust fan   _____   _____

Floors   _____   _____

Lighting requirements   _____   _____

Medicine cabinets   _____   _____

	Rating (0–10)	Comments
Shower stall	_____	_____
Tile	_____	_____
Mirrors	_____	_____

Electricity

Adequate electrical outlets	_____	_____
220-volt outlets for dryer/range	_____	_____
Ample switches	_____	_____
Backup system-generator	_____	_____
Electric utility rates	_____	_____
Lighting fixtures	_____	_____
Outside meter for easy reading	_____	_____

Plumbing

Drainage satisfactory	_____	_____
Hot water heater size	_____	_____
Plumbing fixtures	_____	_____
Public/private sewer system	_____	_____
Quiet operation	_____	_____
Septic system inspection	_____	_____
Utility rates	_____	_____
Sump pump	_____	_____
Water pressure	_____	_____
Water softener	_____	_____

	Rating (0–10)	Comments

Interior Features

	Rating (0–10)	Comments
Number of bedrooms	_____	_____
Guest bedroom	_____	_____
Master bedroom	_____	_____
Built-in bar	_____	_____
Built-in features	_____	_____
Carpeting	_____	_____
Children's play area	_____	_____
Closet space	_____	_____
Curtains	_____	_____
Entrances, sufficient	_____	_____
Family room	_____	_____
Fireplace	_____	_____
Fire/theft alarms	_____	_____
Floor plan logical	_____	_____
Floors solid—few creaks	_____	_____
Free from pest infestation	_____	_____
Ornamental moldings	_____	_____
Privacy of bedrooms	_____	_____
Room size adequate for furniture	_____	_____
Stairs and stair railing sturdy	_____	_____
Sufficient light for house plants	_____	_____

	Rating (0–10)	Comments
Views from windows satisfactory	_____	_____
Washer/dryer— laundry area	_____	_____
Wallpaper	_____	_____

Community

	Rating	Comments
Adequate shopping facilities	_____	_____
Attractive neighborhood	_____	_____
Churches convenient	_____	_____
Flight patterns—aircraft	_____	_____
Garbage and trash disposal	_____	_____
Police and fire protection	_____	_____
Property tax rate	_____	_____
School location	_____	_____
Quality of school system	_____	_____
Special assessments	_____	_____
Street, sidewalks/ lighting	_____	_____
Suitable recreation facilities	_____	_____
Traffic flow, speed limit	_____	_____

GRAND TOTAL _____

No-Frill Homes

In the mid-1970s American manufacturers were quick to respond to the energy crisis by offering consumers stripped-down compact cars as well as compact "no-frill" homes. The public responded enthusiastically by refusing to buy either. As Sol Hurok, the noted impresario, once said, "When the public doesn't want to come, nothing in the world can stop them."

By 1980, steadily increasing gasoline prices and high-cost, hard-to-get mortgage money have finally taken their toll on the inflation-ravaged public. Automobile manufacturers are producing and selling millions of small, light-weight cars while home builders are successfully marketing hundreds of thousands of compact condominiums and no-frill houses. The trend for the future is firmly established.

A few years ago people were moving to smaller homes because they couldn't afford the upkeep of maintaining large homes, heating the rooms, and caring for the yards. Nowadays people are switching to even smaller homes because they can no longer afford the mortgage payments, much less the utilities. At the current rate of progress, in another thirty or forty years we will all be back in caves, sharing them with friends and relatives alike.

At that point, no doubt, some real-estate promoter or advertising executive will come up with a good campaign on the joys of Cooperative Cave Ownership. Of course there will be a full-color brochure pointing out numerous luxury features, such as jogging tracks where you chase the wild animals (or they chase you), built-in sauna (on those muggy summer nights your rocky cave will feel like a sauna), and the interior decoration in *real* earth tones. You won't have to worry about the two- or three-car garage, because the way things are going, there won't be any gasoline left. Enough of the homes of the future.

The no-frill compact homes of today have all the basic ingredients of the frilly homes of yesteryear except for one or two small things: namely, no garage, attic, family room, or basement. There is little landscaping, but the builders, who suggest that you do-it-yourself, usually throw in a free packet of tree seeds.

My wife and I heard of one no-frill home, however, which was advertised as having a "dream kitchen," a huge eat-in, live-in, sleep-in kitchen large enough to meet your every need. *This* was the type of no-frill house that interested us. When we got there we found that the ad was right. You could eat, live, and sleep in that big beautiful kitchen. You had to; it was the only room in the house.

The Best Time of Year to Buy, Sell, or Fall in Love

As there is a time for everything in its season, so too there is a time to buy a home.

If you are fatalistic about where you'll end up living, you could consult your horoscope to see what the stars have in store for you. But if you are interested in getting a good buy on a house, it's best to be on the lookout during the slow season for housing sales.

Ask a real-estate broker which months have the slowest sales activity in your town. Usually housing sales slow down in November and remain slow until March.

During the slumps, sellers rarely see a prospective buyer, and they begin considering the cost of having to heat the house throughout the winter. In colder climates, this consideration, together with the normal mood of pessimism brought on by the ice and snow, chill the seller's hopes of getting a high price.

The seller's enthusiasm is dampened as weeks pass without his seeing a live prospect, and he often drops the price of the house. This is the best time of year for a buyer searching for a bargain.

In most parts of the country (outside the Sunbelt), February is the ideal month for bargain hunters.

Owners of unsold homes who have already moved to other houses have gotten the shock of January's high utility bills for their empty houses and are still afraid that the winter storms may cause costly damage.

When spring arrives with warm breezes, trees budding, and grass turning green, the awakening of Mother Nature brings about a parallel awakening of the seller's hope.

House fever comes on very strong. You can't always safeguard against it. Once you have been bitten by the bug, you'll begin to spend every waking hour thinking of your home-to-be. It's hard to say, "Let's wait for the right time of year." Patience may be a virtue, but it's not an easy virtue.

There is something magical about spring. Just as a

young man or woman's fancy turns to love, so may it
turn to the love of acquiring a better place to live. Besides,
why bother with spring cleaning? It's much more fun to
move.

If you think the bug has bitten you, take heart; there's
plenty you can do about it. If you have a mild case, the
symptoms will be hot, feverish glances through newspaper
ads or a deep sense of malaise whenever you clean the windows. The best prescription is a cold shower. This seldom
cures the fever, but it should leave you wide awake for
the hunt.

If you are still in need of a cure, put up on your refrigerator a big sign that reads, "I am an idiot if I buy a house
before November or after April." This probably won't
stop you either (nothing will in most cases), but it may
moderate the degree of your folly.

If, as spring progresses into summer, you find that re-
current violent attacks of passionate housemania overcome
you, then you are a hopeless case. You might as well accept
your condition and let the disease run its course. I have
discovered that there are several secrets that will work
wonders for you. Secret number one, understood by an
amazingly small number of people, is simplicity itself:
*Do not make an offer on a house unless the listing is
more than two months old or less than two hours old.*

Most sellers understand that it's easier to lower the asking price than to raise it. They ask themselves, "Why not
shoot for the moon?" When a house is first put on the
market, it usually creates a high degree of interest. Flocks

of people come to visit the house: friends, neighbors, competing real-estate brokers, lookers, gawkers, and sometimes a real buyer. All of this activity stimulates the seller's hopes for making a killing on the deal. Often the crowd fails to produce some real "turkey" willing to offer that exorbitant price. Don't you be the turkey.

There is one major drawback to the waiting-it-out strategy. A delightful house which best meets your needs and expectations may come on the market and be quickly snapped up. The house may not have sold at a bargain price, but it might have been the best buy for you because it would have made you and your family the happiest. Don't be so worried about overpaying by several thousand dollars that you lose a really fantastic house. Go ahead and buy it!

But remember, it's hard to be objective if you've got a bad case of house fever. Try to stay away from new listings and wait for one a few months old.

A few sellers naively *underprice* their homes. Usually these sellers just haven't taken the time to study the prices in recent comparable sales. These houses are usually snapped up within a matter of hours, or at most a few days.

Real-estate brokers are often on the lookout for underpriced offerings. As professionals they know the real market value immediately and can make a purchase decision at once.

If you have taken the time to really analyze the market, keep an eye out for these rare bargains. It's like looking for a needle in a haystack. Try not to get stuck and end up buying a lemon at a "bargain" price.

A wise buyer doesn't have to watch the newspaper every day for a new house listing. All that is necessary is to sit back and relax! Look at the listings every month or so and see what hasn't sold for a long time. If one of these houses meets your fancy, that's the time to negotiate for the house. Most houses remain unsold after two months because the listing price is too high. Usually the seller is ready to lower the price at this point. Don't be afraid of missing a great opportunity by not being the first one to see the house after it is listed. The real bargains are found in the slowest selling seasons, months after listing—not in the height of the season, a few days after listing.

Suzanne and I bought our house after it was listed for one week in the peak month for sales.

Secret number two is psyching out the seller. The secret is to have the courage to buy at the worst time of the year. In every area there are certain weeks when the climate is most severe. Wait for heavy snows, ice, torrential rains, mud slides, hurricanes, drought, or other natural disasters, for that is the best time to make your offer.

One of my professors at the Harvard Business School, whose advice has made more than one small investor a big winner, used to explain why most small investors ("small" in dollars invested, not in stature) lose money in the stock market. He pointed out that since small investors don't have a lot of money, they are afraid to lose it. They tend to be cautious when times are bad. If the newspaper announces, "Business is good, but it may not last," the small

investor usually waits to see what will happen before
making up his mind and risking his capital.

As time goes by, the newspapers may report, "Business
conditions are very good and the stock market is rising."
The small investor says to himself, "Yes, I feel better. It's
starting to look good. The time to invest is near."

A little later the papers shout, "The economy is at an all-
time peak. Production and profits are hitting new records.
All signals are go." The small investor says, "This is terrific. I've got to get in on this." And then he buys. This is
usually known as the peak or top of the market.

Once the market starts to drop, the small investor real-
izes that if he sells his stocks he will take a loss. He cau-
tions himself and says, "I won't panic. I will hold onto my
investment until the economy gets better." The market
continues to drop. The economy doesn't get better. The
newspapers say, "A recession is coming, and things look
really glum." The small investor begins to despair. Now
his stocks have lost a substantial amount of their former
value. What to do? He seriously considers selling. It is a
painful step, but one must face facts.

Finally, the newspapers proclaim, "The recession is here,
and in fact things are so bad that a depression could be
right around the corner." At this point the small investor
usually says to himself, "I've lost almost everything; I'd
better recoup something before the end comes." He sells.
This is usually known as the bottom of the market.

There you have it. That is the concise rationale for the
empirically proven fact that the "odd lotter" (a small investor who buys shares in lots of less than 100) often sells

at the bottom and buys at the peak. The name of the game is buy low and sell high, not the reverse.

The same lessons that apply to the stock market also apply to the housing market. The game is won by the courageous. The time to buy is when things look bad. Then people are willing to sell cheap. When times look great and people are bidding up prices, that's the time to sell.

When you are selling your house, just reverse the procedure described in the preceding pages. *Hang on during bad times.*

If buyers fail to show up, hold onto the house. Don't lower the price. A better season is just around the corner. In fact, the best thing you can do is raise the price of your house. Because of inflation, people normally expect houses to get more expensive each year. So don't despair when business is not good. Hold onto your house and raise your asking price.

You may get encouragement from the story of the couple who wanted to buy a house for $50,000. They looked at all the houses in their price range for half a year without finding any they liked. Finally they returned to their real-estate broker and asked to see some houses in the $65,000 category. The broker agreed and then proceeded to show them *the same houses they looked at six months before.*

Stick it out. You may be pleasantly surprised and get a higher price than you originally wanted. This increase can more than make up for any added carrying costs you might have to absorb by holding a house for a few months.

Instead of viewing the slow season as a time of despera-

tion, view yourself as a consummately wise speculator carefully holding onto an investment until the market rises. You may reap a greater gain during the peaking months to come.

Choosing the Right House for Your Children

Have you ever thought, "Sure, I'd like a new house, but we're really buying it for the kids. They're only young for a little while and if we don't buy that house now, it'll be too late"?

Let me break this to you gently. Not many children care about having an impressive foyer or plush apricot carpeting. When was the last time you heard your little ones discussing shades of eggshell enamel or styles of kitchen cabinets? Don't hold your breath and wait for the kids to say, "Gee, Cynthia's house has quarry tile floors and ornate wood moldings. Can we get some too?"

Have you ever stopped to ask your children what color *they* would like to paint the house? Our son opted for dark blue, and we nixed that fast. So what's all this jazz about doing it for them? Kids care about friends, pets, vacation, TV, sex, food, sports, music, and school. They're just not into houses. Every child will tell you that the most exciting house is somebody else's. Kids are into adventure and exploring the world outside their own home. Children are not interested in the style of doorknobs or the shade of your curtains. They're more concerned with basic things like "He's cute," "She's rich," and "I want a pony."

What to Wear When House Hunting

Many sports require specialized gear: good shoes for running, bibs and jackets for skiing, and foul-weather gear for sailing. A house-hunting expedition is no different.

Wear comfortable clothes that will allow you to bend down while looking under sinks or climb easily in and out of cars. Make sure you have big pockets for tape measures, pencils, and note pads. Don't carry large bags that might make you look as if you are about to walk off with the family silver.

Most of us dress for success, though a few achieve it by undressing. When out hunting for a smashing house, many shoppers carefully select clothes that reek of casual elegance and good taste. They choose expensive outfits that reflect their ability to afford a luxurious home. The exact choice varies with the seasons and climate, but usually the overall look suggests that you are just stopping by for a few minutes on your way to the country club.

All of this careful thought and preparation, however, is a complete waste of time. You will soon discover that, invariably, the owner is not home in the first place. Usually the only people who will see you at all are your real-estate broker, possibly a cleaning lady, and the household pets who were left at home to stand guard.

Even though one is always tempted to dress up and "put on the dog," the only one likely to see you *is* the dog. And the dog is apt to greet you by tearing at your nylons, scratching your Amalfi sandals, and grabbing the designer scarf from your pocket. Why go to all that effort to impress a cocker spaniel? Save yourself a lot of time and energy. Wear whatever you like.

In the rare instance when the owner is at home, he is so happy to see a prospective buyer that no matter what you wear, he won't notice it. He will be blinded by the fact that the chance has arrived of finally unloading his over-priced house on anyone, even you.

Bullish on America

Many books have been written on the subject of what to do in view of the so-called impending monetary crisis. Most of these investment guides suggest that you take your cash and convert it to gold or some strong currencies. The experts agree that going out and spending all of your cash as the down payment for a big home, with an even bigger mortgage, is one of the worst things you can do.

But what *fun* is it to be a gold bug? Oh, I guess you could carry around a few coins in your pocket and speak knowledgeably at cocktail parties of your latest maneuvers in the gold market. But these are small pleasures compared to the joys of home ownership.

More and more buyers are going out and purchasing homes that cost more than $100,000. It's fun to mention casually that you have just paid $100,000 for your new home. It would be a lot more impressive if this were your own money.

Why not say, "Well, I borrowed $80,000 and put down $20,000 of my own money (which was all the cash I had left in the world) to buy a house which the bank and I now own together"? It's more enjoyable to make believe we bought our home and "own" it.

A recent buyer was overheard saying, "I had to pay more than $100,000 for my house, but it's worth it!" In reality, he never had $100,000 to pay for anything. Nevertheless, with the lender's help, there he is with a $100,000-plus house. Now all that's necessary is to work hard for the next few years to make the mortgage payments, and then sell the house for a big profit, most likely to someone even poorer. That's the American way.

The most interesting phenomenon associated with the recent surge of inflation-spurred buying occurs when buyers bid up the price of houses to astronomical levels with money none of them has. So off we go, bidding against each other with money we don't have, to buy large homes we don't need.

Housing with a British Accent

Recently Suzanne and I had dinner with a couple who had just arrived from England, Maggie and Nigel Hayden-Davies. We all discovered that the problems connected with owning a home in the U.K. are very similar to those in this country. In fact, the major difference is the vocabulary we use to discuss the same subject.

A single-family home in England is a "detached residence," and a twin single becomes a "semidetached residence." Condominiums are known as "attached housing" and apartments become "flats." An apartment building in England is called a "block of flats" and a row of townhouse apartments is a "terrace." Quite popular are living quarters over a garage or former stables, commonly referred to as "mews." The British don't say "lot," they say "plot," as in "Look at the charming, spacious plots." A housing development in jolly old England is called a "housing estate."

If you are looking for a house with a large yard in England, don't ask for a "yard." The English think a yard is a paved lot where schoolchildren play. What we in America call a yard, the English call a garden. The English "garden" is likely to contain a velvety green lawn, more varieties of annuals, perennials, and herbs than shown in Burpee's spring catalog, plus perhaps a few topiaries in the shape of birds or animals.

The availability of fine housing at reasonable prices is greater in the United States, but the English have compensated for their deficiencies by developing a clearly superior vocabulary.

Imagine Maggie, our English friend in her Harris tweeds, "ringing up" the American real-estate brokerage firm of Hy List and Associates.

She might insist upon a "reception with open views over woodlands and a delightful well-stocked garden." As for location, she fantasizes that a "fine corner position on rising ground, close to the town center and shops," would be desirable, as she anticipates walking to "the greengrocer daily for fresh vegetables."

Our American broker, Hy, is a bit perplexed as he nervously flips through the pages of his multiple-listing book.

"Out here we have something for everyone." Hy continues, "I'm sure we can find the house you describe."

Maggie heeds her husband Nigel's advice to look for a house that gives good value for money.

"Have you any substantial detached houses offering scope for improvement?"

"Oh," Hy replies, "a handyman's special!"

Much to her surprise, he arranges an appointment for her to view several residences on Saturday, Sunday, and the following Tuesday evening. "An assertive chap," she tells Nigel, for in England the offices of estate agents are open only on weekdays during regular business hours.

The best of both worlds would be to live in an American home and speak with a British accent. So let's all get to work. Instead of inviting your friends over to see your "nice spanking-new home," you could invite them to visit "a property of distinction in a much-sought-after position overlooking a favorite reach, complete with velvet lawns and self-contained leisure area." Don't bother to say that you bought your home from a real-estate broker. In England they are called "estate agents."

Remember the Harvard Business School motto: look British, think Yiddish. The British don't live better, they only sound better.

Solar Energy—Bringing It All Back Home

You don't need a weatherman to tell which way the wind blows, but you will need some help to sort through the bewildering proliferation of new product and company names in the solar field. The most creative minds in America have conspired to present us with Solaris, Solaray, Solarmatic, Solarex, Solar King, Solartherm, Solaral, Solargard, Solar-Temp, Solargenics, Solar-Bond, Solar Tran, and Solar Dyne (to mention only a few of the new entries). My personal preference is $olarama.

Now there *is* something new under the sun. Solar engineering jargon is being tossed around at a lot of cocktail parties these days. From coast to coast, energy-conscious consumers are discussing the relative merits of thermal flywheels, rock-bed solar cooling, heat-transfer fluids, flat plate collectors, and variable-speed circulating pumps. This lingo is likely to be with us for a while, so if you feel left out, start to get with it. The Age of Aquarius is here. Instead of flower power, beaded bags, and fringed leather vests, we are "into" regeneration air flow rates and solar hot-water heaters.

You don't have to live in the Sunbelt to benefit from solar heating. Solar collector panels take in energy from the sun's rays. There is enough solar energy to supplement a conventional heating system even when the temperature outside drops below 15°F. As long as it's light outside, some energy from the light rays will accumulate in the solar collectors. (Obviously this system is not so hot in the Land of the Midnight Sun. . . .)

There are two basic approaches to solar heating: "active" and "passive." An active solar heating system requires an array of collector panels to capture the sun's light energy and to convert it to heat energy; a transport system of piping or ductwork to remove the heat from the collectors;

a distribution system to move the heat through the house (very similar to a forced-air furnace); and possibly a heat-storage container of either rocks or liquid. Sound complicated? Well, it's not as complicated as trying to figure out how often the sun will shine, or the efficiency of the system, or the "payback" period.

An active solar system for a new home may cost $10,000 to $15,000, compared to a conventional heating-system cost of approximately $4,000. If fossil-fuel energy prices continue to skyrocket (as most of us expect), the extra investment in a solar heating system may be one of your biggest winners. There is also a federal tax credit now available to those people purchasing active solar equipment, further lowering the initial cost. (See the "Tax Saving Tips" section.)

Passive solar systems utilize nonmechanical means of collecting the sun's energy. A passive solar home might have a solar greenhouse, large windows facing the sun, and heat-absorbing walls, which will bring down the cost of heating conventionally. Other passive devices are reflectors, insulation, and shading screens.

The solar-energy field is still in an early stage of development. Try to locate an architect or builder with previous solar home design experience. Contact other homeowners who are currently living in homes with the system that you are considering and see if they are satisfied with the results. It's fine to jump on the bandwagon early. Just make sure the wagonmaster knows what he is doing, and don't install solar equipment unless you know of a reliable local firm that can service and repair the equipment.

If you are seriously considering solar power, it's wise to learn as much as possible about the principles of solar heat, what system is best for you, and how to make qualified consumer decisions. The best single source of solar literature is the federal government (better than your local electric utility or fuel-oil dealer). The federal government bookstores have a complete listing of all federal publications, from the highly technical to the consumer-oriented "Buying Solar," or write to the Superintendent of Documents, U.S. Government Printing Office, Washington, D.C. 20402.

Once you are in control and can feel the good vibrations (or is that solar flux?), it is time to start shopping for your solar home, or solar-home builder. Contact the National Solar Heating and Cooling Information Center (located in Rockville, Maryland) for a list of solar architects, engineers, and home builders in your area. The National Center also publishes a good bibliography of up-to-date books and articles on the field. The National Solar Heating and Cooling Information Center is operated by the Franklin Institute Research Laboratories for the Energy Research and Development Administration and the Department of Housing and Urban Development.

There's no doubt that solar energy is a red-hot subject. You don't have to be a member of the Sierra Club to imagine the joys of being immune to rising electric, gas, and fuel-oil prices. Saving energy can be difficult, however, and I'd advise hiring an independent third-party solar architect, with no financial interest in designing your house or selling the equipment, to act as a consultant when you are close to a decision about purchasing a solar system.

"This winter our solar home is really paying off"

This is your best chance to get intelligent, unbiased advice. The "payback" period for the consulting fee will probably be shorter than for any solar component you might buy.

Better Homes Than Gardens

The lure of Sirens at sea has caused many ships to dash onto the rocks. Beware the lure of a house with magnificent gardens. Max and Lilly Trillium fell in love with just such a house. The yard had beautiful formal gardens in geometric patterns which captured the spirit of an elegant country manor.

They first visited the home on a sunny summer day. The garden was alive with many varieties of rare roses, begonias, rhododendrons, and a sea of geraniums. When Max looked at the garden for the first time, he did not know the difference between a daffodil and a squash. The owner pointed out the various species in the garden as Max admired the view. "Look over there at the tuberous begonias," she said. Max gazed in the general direction indicated, ashamed to admit that he did not know a tuberous begonia from a dandelion. In addition to the beautiful formal gardens, the house came complete with a heated greenhouse and hundreds of feet of trimmed hedges. The property was surrounded by a dense border of trimmed bushes and towering trees.

There was no question that the garden and greenhouse were the major factors in persuading the Trilliums to buy this house. The grounds were impeccably manicured and gave an air of distinction to their new home-to-be As they gazed upon the grounds in full bloom and in perfect condition, their hearts beat fast.

Looking at the greenhouse on this sultry afternoon, Max could envision a cold winter day when he could go to the greenhouse and see his delicate orchids. The house would have fresh flowers throughout the winter snows. What price can you place on such beauty? The owner of the house explained that in addition to the various plants now blossoming, there were literally thousands of tulip bulbs planted throughout the yard which would bloom in the spring. The lure was irresistible and the Trilliums signed the contract to acquire the house.

In the month between the signing of the contract and the date of their closing, the thought occurred to Max and Lilly that the garden would require some work. Several times during visits to the house they asked the owners for advice on how to take care of the garden. The owners suggested that, at least initially, the Trilliums hire a gardener to maintain the grounds. Lilly asked if they could recommend someone.

"No," they said, "we had some part-time help but we did a lot of the work ourselves."

So she went to work finding a gardener. Soon after the closing but before they took possession of the house, Max arranged for the new gardener, Pete Mulch, to visit the property. As fate would have it, the inspection date was a drizzly, cold, end-of-summer afternoon. The first thing Max noticed as he gazed out upon the garden was that it lacked some of the charm that it had possessed only a

month before. The cold and the rain had destroyed perhaps a third of the blooms. Pete went off by himself
to inspect the grounds and make a checklist of future
requirements.

Max paused to speak with the former owner of the
house. As they exchanged pleasantries, she pointed out
to Max that there was really no reason to worry about all
the leaves that had fallen in the front yard.

"The sycamore trees," she assured him, "are in good
condition and simply have a habit of losing their leaves
and bark a bit early."

Max was nervous. His mind whirled with concerns
about decorating, maintaining the house, and caring for
the garden. Until she had pointed it out, he had not even
noticed that the entire front yard was covered with leaves.
This would not be unusual for a later date, but as he
looked around the neighborhood it was clear that this
front yard was the only one that had leaves. Everyone else's
yard looked impeccable and manicured.

Max ran to the backyard to ask Mr. Mulch to look at
the sycamores. Mulch came over and told Max that the
trees were not sick. "That is simply what sycamores do,"
announced Mulch. This made Max feel the way he felt
the day he explained to an automobile mechanic that his
car was leaking oil, and the mechanic said, "Don't worry,
they all do."

Mr. Mulch then asked Max to come back into the
formal gardens. He took Max to a spot in the backyard
where the grass was turning brown. With his penknife he
pulled up a thatch of sod and showed Max several little

hard-shelled creatures that had made their home in the lawn.

"Cinch bugs," Mulch said. "You've got cinch bugs." Max felt a sharp pain near his heart. Here was the new house he had bought and paid for. Max hadn't even had the pleasure of moving in, only to discover that the cinch bugs were there before him.

"Well," Max said, "surely you can solve this problem."

"No," Mr. Mulch replied, "I just take care of the flowers. The cinch bugs are part of the lawn, and you will have to find a lawn service, unless you intend to take care of it yourself."

Then Mulch explained the careful delineation between the jobs that a lawn service would perform and those jobs that he would perform. A lawn service would rake the leaves, mow, fertilize, and care for the grass itself, whereas he would plant and plan the flower beds, care for the flowers and the greenhouse, and trim the bushes.

"What do you think of our gardens?" Max asked.

Mr. Mulch kept shaking his head and with an amused look said, "You've really got yourself into something, haven't you? You say you're living in an apartment now with only a few house plants and you are going to take care of all this?"

"Well," Max replied, "that's why you're here. I guess I'll need some help."

Pete Mulch smiled, dreaming of the dollars that were to come his way, and said warmly, "We'll be seeing a lot of each other."

"What is the next step?" Max asked him.

"The first thing to do is to get the garden organized. As you see, this garden has many varieties of flowers. It will be necessary to get this down to a manageable level and start planting some low-maintenance flowers that take less work."

"How about these beautiful roses?" Max asked, pointing to a spot where a number of fragile roses stood in their glory.

"Oh, those are rare hybrids that need a great deal of attention," Mr. Mulch explained. "We'd better start thinking of planting some perennials that will take less care."

"Well," said Max, proud to demonstrate his newly acquired knowledge, "can we keep the beautiful rhododendrons and tuberous begonias?"

"Sure we can," Mr. Mulch agreed, "and it might be a good idea," he added, "to see if we can try growing some more of those from cuttings. It may take a little longer to get color in the spring, but it will save you a lot of money."

"How much would it cost," Max asked, "if we just went out and bought some for instant color?"

"Hundreds of dollars each year, if you intend to keep all the annuals you have in your garden presently. The smart thing to do," he advised Max, "is to plant perennials and solve the problem in one fell swoop."

"Well, what does that entail?"

"Probably more than $1,000 for the initial planting, but once that's done you will be off to a good start."

And Max could tell he was off to some start. Mr. Mulch then explained that care for a garden like this would take at least eight hours a week on average, for a thirty-five-

week period. During the busy weeks, tending to this garden would consume at least two or three days a week.
Mulch offered to handle the job for $8 per hour.

"That is, we could keep it to this level if you're willing
to switch to low-maintenance plants and reorganize the
garden."

Max discovered that it was going to cost thousands of
dollars each year just to maintain a garden that possessed
fewer rare blooms than the one he had acquired a month
before.

"Well," Max asked, "how about the greenhouse? Can
we grow some tulips and gladioluses during the cold
winter months?"

Mr. Mulch said, "That sounds a bit ambitious. At least
for the next few years we should content ourselves with
keeping some geraniums in bloom during the winter.
Gladioluses and tulips require 'forcing' and special care,
which would further increase the costs. Of course," Pete
Mulch continued, "your greenhouse will give you the
chance to keep in practice during the winter. That way
you'll be in good shape to work in your garden all summer," he chuckled.

The picture was slowly coming into focus. Max not only
needed a gardener, but also a lawn service. The Trilliums
had acquired not just a beautiful house but also defoliating
sycamores, cinch bugs, and rare flowers that cost thousands
of dollars to keep up and replace. There was no end to it.
As long as the Trilliums stayed there, Max and Lilly would
have the work and expense of keeping up the formal
gardens. One wouldn't want to say that the bloom was

off the rose, but the blooms on Max's roses were literally scattered petal by petal over the brick walk.

Finally, as Mr. Mulch turned to leave, Max asked him, "What about insects and bees? I really don't like bees," Max explained, "and I hoped that there was some way that we could keep them from visiting."

"You may as well face it," Mulch said, "when you have flowers, you'll have bees. You see those big beautiful bushes in your backyard that line the property?"

"Sure," Max said. "What are those?"

"Honeysuckle," Mulch replied. "So you'd better get used to bees. They won't hurt you and you'll learn to live with them."

Feeling wobbly at the knees, Max sat down in his newly purchased garden chair and, in a daze, watched Mulch cheerily patting his wallet pocket as he strolled down the driveway. In the back of his mind, Max could hear a childish little voice piping a familiar tune:

> Mary Mary, quite contrary
> How does your garden grow?
> With silver bells and cockle shells
> And bees and bugs and dough!

How to Buy and Sell
Like an Expert

Adam Smith and the Buyer's
Winning Strategy

Adam Smith, the eighteenth-century economist and author of *The Wealth of Nations,* described the laws of the free marketplace as "the invisible hand." He wasn't referring to something out of *Star Wars.* He had in mind something more powerful than a locomotive, faster than a speeding bullet, and able to leap tall buildings at a single bound . . . *Super Greed.*

He believed that people act mainly to further their self-interest. The force regulating self-interest in the marketplace is *competition:* people charge a high price out of self-interest, and competitors lure people away by charging a lower price. Adam Smith's philosophy of *laissez-faire* recommended allowing this invisible hand to rule the market, the forces of private interests and passions acting in a self-regulating manner.

I'd like to offer some twentieth-century observations and advice on developing a winning strategy in today's marketplace.

For starters, Adam Smith's invisible hand can still be

seen (well, not actually seen, but surely felt). Buyers and sellers are still motivated by self-interest. The seller strives for the highest price he can imagine getting. The buyer wants to pay the lowest possible price. Not much has changed. If you are asked during the course of negotiations why you are being so difficult, just say the invisible hand made you do it.

Adam Smith describes a free marketplace where knowledgeable buyers and sellers meet and act in a rational manner. His economic theory suggests that market forces determine the sales price of a house. That price would be similar to the recent sales prices of "comparable homes."

If one seller asked a very high price, but others are willing to sell comparable homes for less, no one would ever buy the first seller's house. Adam Smith's force of competition is at work.

If the buyer wants to pay a very low price, but others are willing to pay much more for a home, then the buyer will not be able to buy. Each home placed on the market will sell to others willing to pay more.

Thus, in a rational marketplace, the sales price for comparable homes demonstrates the price at which sellers will sell and buyers will buy.

This is the price that Adam Smith would have suggested *you* pay for a house (even though, being a brilliant economist and a savant, *he* lived in rented rooms for years).

A major difficulty in following Adam Smith's theory is securing valid data on recent comparable sales prices. The problem lies in finding houses truly comparable in location, condition, and architecture.

No two houses are identical in every respect. Obviously it's easier to determine a value for your house if it is extremely similar to other homes that have been sold recently.

If you selected a house with many unique qualities, the process of locating comparable sales becomes very difficult.

Collect accurate comparable sales data. Most towns have a Multiple-Listing Service (MLS). This means all real-estate brokers in town who are members of the Multiple-Listing Service have the right to sell the listed house. Contact a real-estate broker whose firm is a member of the Multiple-Listing Service. The member firms receive quarterly published reports, called "comparable books," which provide a summary of sales activity. These reports show listing price, time on the market, and actual final sales prices for houses sold through all multiple-listing realtors. They are your best source of accurate, up-to-date information. Ask your real-estate agent to make the data available to you. The "listing" price is the price the seller starts out asking. That is usually not the same amount that he ends up taking.

Before signing a contract, take the time to research comparable sales. Have your real-estate agent provide you with a written list of comparable sales for the past twelve months in the immediate neighborhood. This list should contain the listing prices and the final sales prices. You'll probably find quite a spread in a number of instances. Don't buy until you verify at least six good comparable sales that support your purchase price. One or two examples may just be flukes.

The chief problem with the multiple-listing books is that they do not provide detailed information on the condition or quality of the house. Often you have to inspect a house, inside and out, to assess value accurately.

How can you be sure your house is actually comparable to the ones in the book without a physical inspection? Each seller usually believes that his house was built with a bit more quality and is therefore worth more than similar houses down the street. In reality, the opposite may be the case.

The only way you have of seeing for yourself the condition of the recent comparable sales is to visit and inspect the houses that have sold. This may sound like a rational approach, but one feels more than a bit foolish calling up your neighbors-to-be. What do you say? "I'd like to visit your house so that I can see how much you overpaid"? A telephone call like this might improve your knowledge of the marketplace, but it would certainly get your name and reputation planted in the new neighborhood where you hope to live!

So, like other prospective buyers, you tend to rely on the information provided by the seller or your own real-estate agent as to the actual interior condition of homes that have been sold recently.

Much of the information you will receive is likely to be hogwash. The seller may not mean to mislead you . . . he is actually convinced that his is the best house on the street, even though this may be far from the truth. If you show interest in a specific house, the real-estate agent may be reluctant to admit that nicer homes in the neighborhood have recently sold for less money than the seller is asking. Many real-estate agents will let you set the tone. They are smart enough not to force their tastes on you. Don't expect them to tell you that the house is an overpriced white elephant. When you describe your latest pipe dream, they will nod and say, "It sounds terrific." If you seem to believe that the price is not *too* far out of line, the real-estate agent will encourage you to make an offer not quite as high as the seller would like, but close enough for the seller to accept. So there you are. No one really did it to you. You did it to yourself!

A second major difficulty with Adam Smith's theory is that he assumed that the marketplace is composed of knowledgeable and rational buyers and sellers. The invisible hand works effectively as long as this assumption is true. Adam Smith was a brilliant economist, and his theory works on a large scale because most of us do act in the manner he describes.

There are exceptions. Some buyers are neither knowledgeable nor rational, but they do buy. Among the ranks of prospective buyers, several interesting types stand out. If you have a house to sell, wouldn't you just love to come across one of that rare species: the out-of-town, rich, unknowledgeable buyer? He's a welcome, if infrequent, visitor to every city. Of course, as advised in the apocryphal recipe for rabbit stew, first you have to catch him.

The Out-of-Town
Rich Unknowledgeable Buyer

Occasionally a buyer new to your city has to acquire a house quickly. He doesn't have time for a thorough investigation of housing prices. Perhaps this buyer is moving

from a city where prices are even higher than in your town.

These buyers may simply say, "Prices seem cheap in this city." If they like a house that is priced well above the actual average comparable market price, they may buy it and believe it's a bargain (a bargain, that is, compared to comparable housing where they came from).

Finding this fellow is the dream of every seller and real-estate agent, but the dread of all other buyers. Out-of-town rich unknowledgeable buyers are in short supply and are currently on the endangered species list.

Be on the lookout for these buyers. If you have sighted one, please proceed with caution . . . he may be armed with a big checkbook and can be dangerous if tempted by a beautiful house.

If you are a prospective buyer who has fallen in love with a house, the rich unknowledgeable buyer is your biggest competitive threat. You may be prepared to make a substantial offer in line with the rational market. Your opponent may be willing to pay a lot more.

The Knowledgeable
In-Town Irrational Buyer

A fairly uncommon member of the society of buyers is the knowledgeable in-town irrational buyer. I myself fall into this dubious category. To join me you must be an individual who (a) has studied the marketplace; (b) fully understands the actual recent comparable sales prices; (c) lives in town; and (d) has fallen in love with a house listed at a high price.

The seller has priced it above the rational market level

in hopes of finding a rich out-of-town ignorant buyer. My type, the knowledgeable in-town irrational buyer, is faced with the slight possibility of losing the house we love to the rich out-of-town unknowledgeable competitor. Confronted with this prospect (totally conscious of the madness of it all), we quickly agree to pay the irrationally high price the seller is asking.

This strategy is akin to pushing the button that starts a nuclear war because (you say to yourself) "if I don't push the button, they may push it first." This has the likely effect of destroying both of you. In the case of the knowledgeable in-town irrational buyer, the strategy only impoverishes him while substantially enriching the seller.

The Buyer's Winning Strategy

If Adam Smith were alive today, he'd take a good look at the housing situation and probably offer the following counsel:

Study the marketplace. Make a list of the recent sales prices of houses truly comparable to the type you want. Go out house hunting for several months before you buy. Some of the homes you visit will sell within a few weeks (probably the ones you liked best). This way you'll know the actual sales prices of homes you had the chance to examine inside and out.

Disregard the occasional extremely high-priced sale that some irrational buyer might have consummated. Rely on average prices of a number of houses.

Equipped with this knowledge, offer no more than 10 percent below the average recent comparable sales price. (This may be 30 percent below the irrational listing price.) In no event offer more than the average market comparable price. Why should you be the one to raise prices for yourself?

The most expensive homes are found in established neighborhoods. These locations may continue to be the best, but they are fully priced today. When you are number one, there's no way to go up, but a long way to drop down. If you are determined to live in the best neighborhood today, be prepared to pay the price for being there.

Your best opportunity for appreciation is to purchase a home in a developing area with high-quality existing homes and stores. Look for a home in the neighborhood where your town's most prestigious department stores have just located their newest branches. If the trend is favorable, and if you will be comfortable living in the neighborhood *while* it is developing, then have at it.

To be successful, you must be willing to risk losing a particular house to some irrational unknowledgeable buyer who may appear. The probability of this is slight. There are few truly irrational buyers, as you can see for yourself by studying the history of the marketplace. If you follow this strategy and do your homework well, you'll be rewarded with the purchase of a fine home at a reasonable price.

How to Make Your Opening Bid

Once you have decided to make a serious offer for a house, the important question is *how much* should the offer be? Most realize that there is a negotiating and a bidding process in arriving at the final price. But what is the best opening-bid strategy?

Keep in mind *Braunstein's First Law of Negotiation: The house you really want is always outrageously overpriced.*

Corollary 1: The owner of the house you really want consistently refuses to lower the price.

Corollary 2: If you hesitate to pay the outrageous price, you will lose the house to another buyer.

Middle-class morality inhibits many Americans from relishing the bargaining process. It doesn't seem right or ethical to negotiate and bargain. Fair dealing dictates that we should accept the price marked on the package. Most of us could learn to improve our negotiating skills by listening to the type of bargaining one might hear in the public marketplace of a distant land. The conversation might sound something like this:

Seller to Buyer: "All I have is yours, my brother, I would ask no more than $200,000 for my home, however poor it makes me."

Buyer to Seller: "How happy I should be if it falls my lot to enrich you by buying your house. I would be pleased to offer $20,000 for your abode."

Seller to Buyer: "Oh, what is this talk of payment between brothers? I need nothing. A payment of only $190,000 would be more than sufficient."

Buyer to Seller: "My only wish is to aid you and your family. If I am to lose money by so doing, it would be honorable. So I am willing to pay you $35,000."

The seller might conclude by saying: "I should have no peace of heart unless I were certain that gain and not loss will be the result to you of buying this house. I'll sacrifice and sell it to you for $187,500."

When bidding for a house, muster up those old poker

skills. First, know your own hand. Then look the seller straight in the eye and bet. If the seller thinks you are bluffing, he will raise and call. Then you'll need more chips and cards before you get that full house. If you play your cards right and keep a poker face, the seller may fold. You could win the hand with a pair of deuces and nerves of steel.

If your offer is very low, it may not be considered seriously. You don't want to lose the house to someone who bids a more realistic price. Don't make the mistake of bidding too much, because your initial bid might be more than the seller is willing to take as the final price. The seller will chortle at hearing your high initial bid, because he knows that you are likely to make one or two higher counteroffers.

It's easy to get carried away during the excitement of bidding. One of my old college poker mates told me how he formulated his initial bid. After finding *the* house, he decided to offer $90,000. When he was finally ready, he called the owner. Just as he began to make the opening bid, he heard himself offering $100,000. As he related to me, "I just couldn't bring myself to say the lower number." He still didn't manage to buy the house. It was snapped up by another buyer who couldn't resist bidding more. Many sellers rely on the maxim "There's a sucker born every minute." Sometimes there are two.

In the event that you *are* the highest bidder and do buy the house, there is little doubt that you have become a prime example of *Braunstein's Second Law of Negotiation: Nobody else would have ever agreed to pay as much as you have.*

How to Sell Your Home for
<u>More</u> Than It's Worth

I'd rather be a buyer than a seller. In fact, it's almost impossible to enjoy selling your home. If the house sells quickly, you will spend the next few years kicking yourself for giving it away at a ridiculously low price. If the house stays on the market for many months, the agony is unbelievable! The only way to achieve a clear-cut victory is to sell the house quickly for double its highest imaginable value to some rich ignorant buyer. The odds of doing this are somewhat akin to discovering oil while tilling your garden.

Beware of the standard advice given by most *How to Sell Your House for Fun and Profit* books. Typically, these books advise you to hold a garage sale, keep your house spotless, repaint when necessary, and don't under- or overprice your house. These suggestions all sound logical, but I'm not so sure they make much sense.

Let's take a look at some of the so-called experts' ideas. What about holding a garage sale, for instance? Garage sales usually do attract attention. Your friends and neighbors will arrive in droves to clamor over the goodies. When it's all over, you will have succeeded in selling some junk. Don't get carried away with enthusiasm for the sale and sell off any "good" junk that you'll regret parting with for years to come. When you total the loot, the net profit is likely to be $37.29.

In the process, you have worn yourself to a frazzle dealing with the sale. It's not too farfetched to imagine that some prospective home buyer might drive by your house during the garage sale and leave with a less-than-great impression. Unless you actually enjoy playing junk dealer for a day, forget the advice about holding a garage sale.

Instead, if you have some household goods you're certain that you want to dispose of, donate them to a worthwhile charity. You will avoid all the hassles of a garage sale, take a tax deduction based on the value of the items, and help some people in need.

Another piece of worthless "good advice" is the admonition to keep your house spotlessly clean. This challenges the ingenuity and fortitude of the most energetic seller. Usually real-estate brokers call to give you five minutes' notice that they are on the way over with a possible buyer. This occurs most often when you are in the middle of either cooking dinner, fingerpainting with the children, or cleaning a backed-up sink that has quit working until the plumber arrives.

If your broker *does* give you a day's advance notice for a showing, the chances are pretty good that after you have spent hours waxing and polishing they won't show at all.

When broker and buyers do arrive, it's often for a sixty-second tour because the prospective buyers decided as they first pulled into the driveway that your house doesn't appeal to them, with or without the dust.

Unless you are one of those people who *really* hates dirt, relax and don't worry about a little sloppy housekeeping.

The couple who eventually buy the house probably can't stand your wallpaper, think that the drapes are tacky, and wonder how you ever lived with that dreadful carpet in the living room. But they see real possibilities in the house, love it anyway, and feel that they must have it. Do you actually think a little dust will stand in their way?

Most guides to selling your home recommend against any last-minute expensive remodeling work, but they do suggest sprucing up the house with a coat of paint.

I suspect that during this past year, two million American families repainted at least some rooms in their homes in preparation for a sale. Shortly afterward, another two million American families who bought those homes repainted those same rooms because they couldn't stand the color.

Homes that change hands several times within a few years have been known to have a half-dozen layers of paint on the walls. Nobody likes the other fellow's decorating scheme.

This six-layer paint-and-paper caper is an unbelievable boon to the paint manufacturers of America. I'd advise you to take the proceeds from the sale of your house and open a paint store. It's a hell of a business!

The only example of sillier human behavior that I can think of is the practice American men have of wearing suits and sports jackets with those little buttons on the sleeves. I've been wearing them for years and have never figured out what the buttons do, except fall off.

Imagine all those buttons. If 75 million American males each have two coats with three buttons per sleeve, we are going around as a nation with 900 million buttons we don't need. And this doesn't begin to count the British, French, Germans, or Swiss.

Another vicious falsehood perpetrated by the guys who make a fast buck on how-to-sell-your-house guidebooks is the old saw *Don't overprice your home.* This is pure rubbish. These "experts" are quick to point out that the overpriced house will probably remain on the market for quite a time. They also suggest that would-be buyers will conclude that there must be something wrong with it, if the house has been on the market for a long while. Any fool can easily tell that the only thing wrong with the house is that the price is too high . . . an easily correctable condition any time the seller wishes to lower the price.

W. C. Fields said, "Never give a sucker an even break." P. T. Barnum proclaimed, "There is one born every minute." Why not take the time and try to find a foolish buyer who will pay you thousands more than your house is worth?

A few buyers will find that your house has all the special features they desire. Some people will fall in love with everything from your avocado-colored refrigerator to the foil wallpaper in the guest bathroom. To those buyers, your house is worth thousands more than the average selling price. Many buyers spend a fortune redecorating once they are in their new home. If the buyers find a perfect fit, they'll pay those thousands to you.

Some buyers just don't take time to shop the market. They might like your house and pay top dollar.

Once in a while, a rich out-of-town buyer will come in

and substantially overpay for a house. It should only happen to you; and it might if you have patience.

It's likely that you will have to wait a long time to find the right buyer. So what! Most homes are on the market less than three months before they're sold. Why be in such a hurry to give your house away within ninety days at an average price? You took months to find the house. You have spent thousands of dollars and possibly years maintaining and decorating your home. *Don't panic and sell it too fast.*

However, don't get so carried away with your expectations that you'll wind up feeling like my friend Harry. Harry went off the deep end and decided to ask $100,000 for his house (which was worth $60,000 tops). His grandfather heard this and called him up.

"Harry," the old man began, "I know a man who will give you $150,000 for your house."

"Terrific," said Harry in a state of high excitement. "Who is he?"

His grandfather sighed. "The same man who will give you $100,000."

People who are otherwise rational, sane, witty, and wise tend to fall apart at the seams when the time arrives to sell their house.

Throughout America, millions of sellers are running around working hard at holding garage sales that bring in less than $100, while trying in a panic to sell their most valuable possession, their house, within a short time. Most end up selling to the early bidder at a mediocre price.

To bring this about, the well-meaning but often bumbling sellers can be seen hard at work scrubbing and polishing floors or painting rooms that most buyers will dislike and immediately repaint.

If you see a bleary-eyed couple driving around aimlessly in the family car, with the rear seat filled with screaming children and barking dogs, chances are they are hiding out during an "open house" showing of their home.

But what would you expect from a civilization that goes around wearing 900 million useless buttons?

Whatever Goes Up Must Come Down?

Recently a little girl wrote a letter to the business editor of her local newspaper.

Dear Sir:

I am eight years old and all of my friends tell me that whatever goes up must come down. I won't believe it's true unless you tell me so.

Your friend,
Virginia

The harried editor took time out of his hectic schedule to reply:

Dear Virginia:

Your friends are not telling you the truth. Not everything that goes up must come down. For instance, mortgage interest rates keep going up and up.

Although in the short term these interest rates may decline, long-term trends indicate a continued upward movement. The chief cause of this is inflation. While the rate of inflation may decline, all this really means is that prices keep going up, only slower.

Yes, Virginia, some things like inflation may always be with us. Do not despair, for so long as there is truth and beauty in the world Santa Claus will always be with us too. But the presents he brings will continue to cost more and soon Santa may be able to come only every other year.

Sincerely,
M.B.

How to Get a Good Deal on a Mortgage Loan

Last spring ZsaZsa and Mort Gagor searched the marketplace for a good deal on a loan.

Mort began with his local S & L, the Big Spread Savings & Loan Association, where he had his savings accounts. Mort was a racquetball buddy with the treasurer of the S & L, Eli Quid.

"Well, Eli," Mort began, "my wife and I have found a terrific new house we'd like to buy."

ZsaZsa Gagor was hoping that she would be able to move out of her snug ten-room cottage and into something less cramped.

"How about it, Eli?" Mort continued. "What's your best preferred rate for a good loyal customer like me?"

"Let me talk with our president, Mr. 'Points' Cassidy, and we'll let you know what we can do," Eli responded brightly.

A few minutes later Eli returned, looking less eager.

"Sorry, Mort. We really can't do a bit better than our regular rate."

Mort then decided to shop and compare this rate with other lenders in town. He was smart enough to realize that it rarely makes sense to shop for a home loan at an out-of-town lending institution, unless the firm's president happens to be your brother-in-law. The reason is that the out-of-town banker is not familiar with real-estate prices and values within your town. The lender therefore is nervous, uncertain as to the value of your property and the desirability of the location. As a result, the loan officer tends to be more conservative and prefers to lend a smaller percentage of the purchase price. In addition, an out-of-town lender would wonder why you are going outside your community to shop in the first place. Perhaps your standing in your hometown isn't what it should be.

Now that you know where to shop, let's review what features you want in a mortgage loan. The most important factors are: first, the amount of money you can borrow (this is the critical factor if you are like most folks today and can't really afford the house you're buying); second, the interest rate and any points or fees that you may be charged for the loan; and third, the term of the loan. Your assignment (if you care to accept it) is to get a long-term, low-interest loan, for a high percentage of purchase price.

Savings-and-loan associations are the largest source of residential mortgage money. In addition to supplying conventional mortgages, lenders may be able to arrange mortgages insured by the Federal Housing Administration (FHA) in the amount of 90 to 95 percent of purchase price. If the buyers are armed-forces veterans, they may qualify for a Veterans Administration (VA) insured loan with no money down. It is necessary to contact the local VA office to determine eligibility. You might want to ask the lender about private mortgage insurance. If it's available, the cost of the loan is a little higher, but lenders will lower their conventional down payment requirements.

When Mort was shopping for a loan, he decided to try out several negotiating strategies. First, he told his friend Eli at the Big Spread Savings & Loan that he would have to withdraw all his savings funds if they wouldn't give him a deal a little better than the going market rate. This approach met with no success. (I'm sure the bankers suspected that Mort would soon withdraw all his savings anyway just to pay for the furnishing and upkeep of the house . . . a shrewd guess on their part.)

Next, he went to other banks and savings associations in town, offering to establish a new "passbook" savings account (the most profitable type for the financial institution because it pays the lowest rate of interest) in return for a special low rate on a loan. This approach also met with failure. No one wanted to lower a long-term mortgage rate for a short-term deposit. (What did you really expect?)

The problem is that lenders all seem to charge about the same rate at any given time. Lenders also have similar ideas as to term and amount. When the haggling is done, you really end up with about the same deal at any bank or savings institution.

The most important lesson is that getting a good deal on a loan depends more on the time when you are trying to borrow funds than on any special deal you are likely to negotiate with a lender. It's the old law of supply and demand.

When loan demand is low, financial institutions have large cash reserves and are eager to make loans. That is the time to be shopping for a new house.

When money is tight, financial institutions are paying high interest on deposits, and loan demand from prospective borrowers like yourself is high. Then lenders can charge high interest rates, demand points, and lend a low percentage of purchase price.

During the current times of tight money and high mortgage interest rates, you should consider these several alternative approaches to financing. First, try to get the seller to finance the purchase by accepting your note as part of the purchase price. If you can't scrape together a down payment (in tight money times lenders require larger down payments), ask the seller to accept your second mortgage note as part of the down payment. Sellers are aware that the money crunch works a hardship on all buyers, and the seller may be willing to give you a below-market interest rate to get the house off his hands.

Second, if you are buying a house with an existing FHA or VA mortgage, you should be aware that these loans are assumable. But FHA and VA do not allow second mortgages, so be prepared to come up with a large cash down payment if you want to assume a low-interest existing mortgage on a house with an appreciated equity value.

"Even if we are willing to stick our necks out,
it doesn't look like there's much left!"

Soon after your meeting with the friendly banker, he finally acquiesces and agrees to make a loan. He charges you the highest rate of interest ever recorded in the history of the United States for a home loan mortgage. On top of that rate, you might also pay an additional point or more for getting the loan (which doesn't sound like much until you have to write the check).

To most of us, after months of emotional commitment to finding a new house, the thought of being unable to buy it, regardless of the cost of money, is completely unacceptable. Crazy as it sounds, you will find yourself thankful because the lender is the one who is making this transaction possible.

I'll bet that you will look him in the eye, shake his hand, and gushingly (even sincerely) thank him for making the loan.

ZsaZsa and Mort got their loan, too. And they're paying the same rate as the rest of us.

What Really Happens at a Real-Estate Closing

As the closing day approaches, the sellers of the house spend their time on the telephone pleading with the gas company to perform an inspection. A termite inspection by a reputable company is also usually required by the buyers to confirm that no such creatures lurk in the floorboards. Armed with letters from the gas company and Orkin, the world's largest termite exterminator, the sellers are ready to certify that their house will neither blow up nor fall down.

The legal abstract or record of title of the house is now making its way from the seller's vault to the seller's attorney to the buyer's attorney and finally to the officer in charge of closings at the lending institution making the mortgage loan. This examination of the abstract is necessary to assure the buyers and bank that the seller, and not the Seminole Indians, has good title to the property. As the abstract moves along its way, the progress is followed and noted by the eager buyer, who wants to be certain that everything will be in order.

Now is the time to learn that it is easier to put money into a bank than to get it out. One buyer I knew contacted his savings bank to ask for cash or a certified check.

(If a certified check is required at closing, make certain it is payable to yourself. This way you can either endorse it over to the seller, or keep it if a problem arises at closing.)

The banker informed him that they would be happy to issue a check on their bank, but that savings institutions could not issue certified checks.

"Well," said the buyer, "just give me the cash." The bank officer replied, "I'll be back in a minute." He came back a few minutes later looking rather embarrassed. "I'm sorry, but we don't have the cash."

"This is incredible," said the buyer. "What is the size of your bank? How much do you have on deposit?"

"Well," the banker replied, "we have $100 million in deposits but we manage our money very efficiently. That money is invested at all times and at the moment we don't have $40,000 in cash." Then the loan officer put the buyer in a calmer mood by noting that the lender's check would no doubt be accepted at the closing. It is good to plan in advance if you must have cash or a certified check available.

In the event of another Great Depression in this country, we really don't have to worry about having a "run" on the banks. Given the amount of actual cash available at most lending institutions, it would be more like a "walk."

As a matter of fact, one little old lady would probably withdraw all her deposits in cash and that would be it for the day.

There are numerous "hidden" closing costs that further deplete the buyer's checkbook. The federal government enacted the Real Estate Settlement Procedures Act (RESPA) to help protect buyers from last-minute surprises. This act doesn't lower the closing costs, but it does require the mortgage lenders to give buyers notice prior to the closing date so that they can have time to try to scrape together some extra cash. The amount of these closing costs can vary a great deal, but it is not unusual to have them total $1,500 or more.

Here is a list of various costs and fees that might be incurred at closing. Most lenders would not require every item:

1. Mortgage application fee
2. Loan origination fee
3. "Points" or up-front loan discount fee
4. Credit investigation fee
5. Mortgage insurance application
6. Hazard insurance premium
7. Title insurance
8. Bank attorney

9. Appraisal and survey fees
10 Lender's inspection fee

It's a good idea to ask the lender for an estimate of closing costs *before* you make the loan application. That way you know how much you have to borrow!

The closing ceremony has many similarities to a wedding. After love at first sight, courting, and proposal, we come to the grandest day of all with mounting anticipation. One goes to bed thinking of a million trivial things. What type of clothes are appropriate for a closing? Where is the good pen? Will the baby-sitter be on time? And most important, where is the checkbook?

The day finally dawns and it is a beautiful one. The buyers set out for the bank. Once at the bank they are faced by a crowd of people—the sellers, the attorney for the sellers, the real-estate brokers, the buyers' attorney, the banker, and his assistant.

In most instances, the sellers look as glum as the bride's parents. It is with mixed emotions that they attend. They are happy to get rid of the house and receive the cash, but sad to lose the home where they have shared so many happy moments.

The buyers, on the other hand, particularly when it is their first house, are elated, yet bewildered by the onslaught of papers (mortgage, note, closing statement, deed, etc.) presented to them for inspection and signature. The banker makes buyers and sellers alike raise their right hands to swear that they are signing all these documents under their own free will. Everybody at this point is harboring their most knowledgeable and efficient expressions. The whole occasion is permeated by a most ridiculous sense of solemnity.

After the second time we had to raise our hands to swear to something or another, my wife Suzanne finally broke the tremendous tension by saying, "Wait, I only swore because my husband kicked me under the table." Our attorney quickly assured us that the banker would thoroughly examine everyone's shins at the end of the closing, to ascertain whether or not they signed the documents of their own volition.

The buyers usually present a check to the bank for a sum ranging from 10 to 25 percent of the purchase price. The bank then gives the sellers a check for the total amount of the purchase price.

Our attorney jokingly admitted that during the closing of his own house, the emotional stress was so great that he had to rewrite his check three times. I smiled at him benignly while proceeding to write my check and omitted the ever-so-important word *thousand* on the dollar line.

The attorney for the buyers has very little to do at the closing. One of his few possible tasks is to read aloud to the buyer the provisions of the mortgage. Usually the attorney prefaces this reading by saying to the buyers, "This is the most important step you are about to take in your entire life and I want you to understand fully what it is that you are doing. Let me read to you the exact provisions of this mortgage so that you will understand what you are signing."

He states that the buyers agree to borrow the funds and

pay them back, and that there are many bad things that can happen to them if they don't pay the money back. The buyers already know, deep inside, that it is madness to spend all this money for a house. God only knows who will pay for it if they get sick or laid off. So at a time like this they really don't need to have their attorney read out loud the nasty provisions of the mortgage.

The bank won't change the provisions regardless of what your attorney says. It is a standard form of mortgage that has not been prepared especially for you, but for every other home buyer. Nothing your attorney can say is likely to change it. *If you want to change the form of mortgage, buy the bank, not the house.*

In a room full of people, you are not about to back out, take your money, and walk away after all the months of aggravation merely because your attorney is pointing out that in the event of default on the mortgage the bank can wipe you out.

I knew one young attorney who had the proper sense of humor about all this. At the closing, he would pick up the mortgage and instead of reading the nasty provisions about the way the bank could wipe out the borrower, he read the provisions about the "grace period." It says that if you don't make the payment on time, the bank is obligated to give you a grace period of so many days (usually thirty days) before it can begin foreclosure. So the young attorney would read in a slow and reassuring manner and tell his clients to relax, because if they couldn't cough up the money for their mortgage payment, there was nothing that the bank could do about it for a while.

The attorney for the sellers has even more difficulty finding something to do at the closing because it is not his role even to review the mortgage. At a recent closing, the sellers were represented by Sam Charge, Esq., a partner in the law firm of Bicker, Procrastinate & Charge. Sam had only one opportunity to play some small role (which he eagerly awaited) when the officer of the bank asked the owners, "Are there any liens or unpaid bills that you know about?"

At this point Sam jumped up and said to his clients, "Now this is very important. Are you sure there are no liens or unpaid bills that you know about?"

The sellers of the property always reply, "Yes, we are sure everything is all right."

The attorney for the sellers says to the loan officer, "Yes, we have checked, everything is fine." And thus ends the major role of the attorney for the sellers.

The real-estate broker's role at the closing is also largely ceremonial. Each broker will work to prepare a separate closing statement. (A closing statement is a complete financial accounting of all disbursements, expenses, and prorations related to the sale.) But the lender has his own statement and this is the one that is used to disburse checks. The only mathematical calculation that is really important to the brokers is the one in which the sellers take the sales price, multiply it by the rate of commission, and give them a check for that amount.

Everything is signed, and the first person to leave is the lender. He probably is heading for the closest chapel to pray that his borrowers are as solvent as he has been led to believe and that the house is actually worth as much as the appraised value. The real-estate brokers leave with their commission checks in hand, on their way to the million-dollar round table. The attorneys leave happy in the knowledge that they can now go home, send out bills, and receive their fees for services rendered.

The sellers leave with a check in hand, eagerly awaiting a chance to spend the loot. Often the poor sellers need this money for a down payment on the next house, which they have already purchased, most likely with an even bigger mortgage. In all likelihood, the sellers also get to keep the house for the next thirty days until the buyers finally get possession. The vacancy date of sellers is a negotiable provision of the contract, but most often the eager-to-please buyers readily agree to give the "poor" sellers time to pack up and leave.

The buyers are allowed to stay longer in the conference room of the bank because they are too stunned to get up. They have no money and no place to go. Thank heavens for the real-estate agent who wants to take them out to lunch to celebrate the closing. But who has time for that? It is usually necessary to rush back to the office and make enough money to meet the first mortgage payment.

Between Contract and Possession

As the moving date approaches, the novice homeowner will need to figure out what to do in the new house when: the

"My gosh! We'll need all of these people
to keep this place going?"

furnace stops working; the lights flicker and die; a section of spouting falls down; the bees build a hive next to the bedroom window; that slow water leak in the basement starts to speed up; the grass turns brown.

During moments like these, it is helpful to have a list of people to call for assistance. You'll also need a basic understanding of where the "mechanicals" in your home are located. A good step would be to meet with the present owners, prior to closing if possible, because they certainly will be more interested in spending some time with you *before* they get your check.

Ask the owners to help you compile a list of all the various contractors, plumbers, electricians, maintenance personnel, and so forth, who have been called in over the years. While you're at the house, it's a good idea to take a guided tour of the mechanicals. Learn where your air-conditioner compressor and fuse box are located, how to turn your furnace on, and where to shut the water and gas off.

When you first visited the house, the thought might have occurred to you that it would be a good idea to examine carefully what you were buying. In the frenzy and excitement of real life, rarely does one make the decision to buy a house *after* learning how everything in it works. Now that you are committed and about to take charge, how about calling up the present owner? Get right over there for a little help and some sound advice.

The Art of
Home Improvement

Remodeling Made Simple . . . Don't!

New homeowners have the energy and enthusiasm to knock down walls, remodel rooms, paper, paint, carpet, and decorate. After we've been in the house for a few years, most of us can hardly find the energy to make the bed and take out the garbage.

Remember *Braunstein's First Law of Home Improvement: Everything you do will cost more and take longer than you expect.* Come to think of it, this applies not only to remodeling but to almost everything else you do as well.

Until recently many savvy homeowners simply sold their existing houses and "traded up" to buy better homes rather than endure the woes of remodeling.

Today's money crunch sky-high interest rates are causing thousands of homeowners to consider keeping what they have. Few of us are hot to give up a good old-fashioned 7 to 9 percent mortgage for the pleasure of financing the purchase of a new house at the current high rates.

The newest trend is to keep your present home and remodel it. This approach should be used as a last resort only after you have tried Zen, needlepoint, gin rummy, crossword puzzles, and Rolfing.

If you can't stand your home as it is another minute,

but think you'll be satisfied with a *minor* remodeling job (actually there is no such thing), then see your friendly loan officer. Arrange a second mortgage home improvement loan to finance the work, unless you have the cash already saved up. If you do have the cash, please keep in mind *Braunstein's Second Law of Home Improvement: Any remodeling project you can afford without obtaining a new loan is too insignificant to make you happy.*

Financing an addition with a home improvement loan will probably cost several percentage points more than current mortgage interest rates. (When you add this up, you'll probably find out that it's cheaper to use Master Charge.) The advantage of the home improvement second mortgage loan is that you will be able to keep your present *low* first mortgage rate intact.

Don't underestimate the cost of your remodeling job. Take your estimate, double it, and hope this will suffice. I'm sure you've heard this all before and you don't believe it can happen to you. That's what everyone else thought, too. There are two good reasons why we all make the same mistake: too much optimism and not enough experience. If you can't afford to spend double the amount you're presently estimating, don't start the project. Naive human optimism cries out, "It might have happened to others, but it will not happen to me because I'll plan ahead." That's what Napoleon said about the Russian winters.

The desperate anxiety of finding a house is nearly matched by the disheartening task of trying to get workmen to come to your home. Are you really ready to go through that sort of fuss all over again?

If you don't put a strict limit on those expensive re-modeling ideas, you won't be able to afford a stick of new furniture. You may want to sacrifice some improvements for a while in favor of having something to sit on. How long can you keep telling your friends and relatives that the house is still empty because the furniture is on order? (Actually, with deliveries so slow, this ploy is probably good for six months to a year.) The time has arrived to stop dreaming up improvements and stay within your already strained budget.

Before starting major remodeling plans, ask your attorney to investigate any deed restrictions or zoning ordinances that might stop you from making additions. Zoning ordinances frequently establish front, side, and rear setback requirements that might hinder your plans for a nifty three-car garage, tennis court, or swimming pool. Don't be too upset if these restrictions force you to give up your plans. It's probably the best thing that could have happened. Instead, take the money and go on a relaxing vacation.

If you're still determined to go ahead and remodel, let me give you a few insights on what lies ahead. Be pre-pared for days of sitting alone in your home waiting for workmen who will never arrive. You'll have the pleasure of making futile calls to ask, "Where are the men and why haven't they arrived?" This is invariably answered by "They are out and we can't reach them. They'll call back tomorrow." Usually they don't.

Your best chance for success in contacting repairmen is to follow the advice of our cheery hot-and-cold-running plumber Jocko Malloy, who let us in on the secret. He advised,

> "Early to bed,
> Early to rise,
> It's the only way
> To contact the guys!"

Start making calls at seven in the morning. Many contractors work out of their homes and leave early to be on the job (some other job, not yours). If you want to be successful at scheduling work, your pleading and begging must be done between seven and seven-thirty.

Most contractors are vague about the time when they will come. "Next week" or "Next month" are common replies. You'll never hear them say, "Tomorrow" or "How about four o'clock on the thirteenth?"

To give you an idea of the remodeling game, here's what happened one morning at our dream house.

My schedule was simple. Casual laborers were to arrive early to haul out debris from the bedroom wall we wanted knocked down. At the same time, our friendly neighborhood electrician Antonio "Flash" Giordano had promised to remove the wiring from the doomed wall. Later, one of Ma Bell's minions was to arrive and install a new telephone line in the bedroom. Then, to complete the picture, a company advertising itself as the "fastest lay in town" was to send carpet installers to lay carpet in the living room.

And what were the results? Well, the casual laborers didn't show. Neither did Flash Giordano. I was almost ready to tear out my hair by the time a knock at the door signaled the arrival of the telephone repairman. He looked around and explained that he couldn't install the phone until the electrician moved the wiring, so he left. Then, to top off the day, the carpet installers came. They took one look at the job, decided that they didn't have the right materials, and walked out.

While leaving, one of them asked, "Do you want to sell your car?" (They probably get a lot of positive replies to questions like this from broke homeowners.) He then suggested that if it were his home he wouldn't put down carpets at all. He promised to return "tomorrow, maybe." He didn't.

When the casual laborers did show up, the only thing casual was their work, not their price. And you still want to remodel your house?

When you eventually find an excellent contractor, you will want him to stay forever. The emotional dependency that grows between an anxious homeowner and a good finish carpenter is closer than many mother/son relationships. We're seriously thinking of adopting our carpenter, even if he is older than we are, and married.

Don't settle for poor workmanship. Most contractors are capable of first-class work. If you see something that doesn't look right to you, call it to their attention immediately. If you are a novice homeowner uncertain what to look for, hire an architect to inspect the work.

I had mixed results in challenging their pride to inspire them to high-quality work. One approach I tried was "Please don't do anything for me that you wouldn't be satisfied with yourself." This was interpreted by them as a sophisticated form of nagging. Most of the men have wives who carry around lists of unfinished at-home tasks.

A better approach was "If man can send a rocket to the moon, certainly he can figure out how to install a stair railing that doesn't shake." This produced good results. Our stair rail no longer shakes, but the contractor's bill was only a little less than NASA's budget.

Remodeling jobs can range from installing a modern faucet on an old sink to building an enormous addition as big as your existing home. All remodeling jobs, large or small, have several things in common. They are all more difficult, time-consuming, and expensive than they initially appear. But it is immensely satisfying to see the job through to completion. It gives you an insight into Sir Edmund Hillary's feelings when he reached the summit of Everest.

Many remodeling jobs first appear to be simple procedures that any well-intentioned amateur do-it-yourselfer could complete in an afternoon. This is a delusion. You will be able to learn as you go, but you won't know what you need to know at the point when you need to know it.

Try to meet others who have already done it. This advice could apply equally well to skydivers, mountaineers, or wing walkers in an air circus. You will want all the help you can get.

Renovating an old house is a lot like opening Pandora's Box. Simple jobs easily snowball into major undertakings. Perhaps you'd like to take off those old asphalt shingles and expose the charming clapboard siding underneath. Once you have ripped off half the asphalt shingles, you'll probably stop and discover that the clapboard siding is broken and cracked. After you have pulled off the siding, you'll notice that the sills are shot and half the house needs to be rebuilt.

Several months and many thousands of dollars later you might begin to wonder what was so bad about asphalt shingles in the first place.

Some old houses are literally held together with dirt, leaves, and caulking compound. Shine up the place and it may fall apart before your eyes. There are so many variables and unknowns that it is hard to estimate cost and time for renovation. Professional contractors are reluctant to bid this type of work without an enormous margin built in for contingencies. They'll probably need it.

It's hard to hire professional general contractors. The few well-known firms with reputations for quality work and fair prices are booked up so far in advance that you'll probably move to another town by the time they could fit you in. If you have house fever and want the work done yesterday, the quickest way to proceed is to become your own general contractor. Pick up the Yellow Pages and start calling the subcontractors you'll need—plumbers, carpenters, electricians, drywall men, concrete firms, roofers, and tile installers.

Hire an architect to review the subcontractors' initial bids for proper specifications and to inspect their work. You may not think you're able to afford the architect, but you can't afford not to have him. Architects are usually not as busy as well-qualified remodeling general contractors (that must tell you something), so you shouldn't have any problems finding an architect who will come over quickly.

Delays are inevitable. When your subcontractor comes to you with a good sob story, be ready for him. Have a good sob story of your own prepared in advance.

Your carpenter will say, "I can't make it because I've run into problems at the job I'm at now. It looks like another three or four weeks till I can break loose." Hit him hard with "If you're not at my home by this afternoon, I'll place ads in the newspaper stating that your firm fails to live up to its promises. It may cost some money, but I'll have the satisfaction of letting thousands of homeowners know what it's like trying to do business with you!"

Your plumber will say, "I can't come over because it's snowing, I have the flu, and my Cadillac is stuck in a drift." At this point you should have a rapid reply set to go. Begin with "Our family doctor insists that we finish this remodeling job immediately. The children are ill from constant exposure to sawdust and debris. So either come over today, or pay *our* doctor bills."

You could suggest to the plumber that you won't give him any more business in the future if he doesn't come right over. This gambit usually elicits uncontrollable laughter, but no plumber.

If you're tempted to threaten to call another plumber, save your breath. Several hours of phone calls will convince you that it takes weeks to get the next plumber, if *he* lives up to his promises.

The electrician may say that he'll be a few days late because his truck isn't working. He really means "I've found some poor sap who is willing to pay me triple time to do his job first."

Remodeling jobs are more difficult to finish than they are to start. Months after the work is almost complete, there's always some small unfinished detail—one last piece of baseboard that never was replaced; some hardware for the cabinets; or those attractive electrical plate covers and switch plates that are still on order. Perhaps you still can't find the right lighting fixture for the new bath; or there's some matching trim molding yet to be installed.

When the job is almost over, you will probably discover that you forgot to: put in enough closet space; install light switches near the door to the room; provide easy access to new plumbing; install an adequate number of well-placed heat and air-conditioning vents; or run pipe for outside water faucets. If by some miracle you remembered all of the above, I'll bet you could write your own list.

Superman's X-ray vision doesn't compare with the new special remodeler's vision you will acquire after working on the job. The average myopic homeowner suddenly discovers that he can spot a minor flaw at twenty yards. The three-martini lunch is the only known cure for this oversensitivity to minor flaws.

Tools of the Trade

Have you seen the tape measure, dear?
Is a cry you are likely to hear
From a mate in distress
Who will cause great unrest
If that tape measure doesn't appear.

The average tape measure seems to disappear faster than a cold beer on a warm night in a campus dorm. It's never there when you need it.

An epidemic of "Tape Measure Bulge" is sweeping the country. Patients are exhibiting such symptoms as an irregularly shaped bulge that protrudes from areas of the body in the vicinity of pockets. To paraphrase a famous Mae West line: "Is that a tape measure in your pocket or are you happy to see me?"

Even after the swelling has subsided, permanent damage sometimes remains in the form of stretch marks and baggy pockets.

The disease may be cured by leaving your tape measure in the drawer and carrying a yardstick at all times.

Today's household hint is to measure some part of your anatomy so that you can measure without a tape. For instance, measure the size of your foot, the length of your longest stride, or the span of your outstretched fingers. When you need to measure something for the house, just whip out your foot or finger and use it instead. Soon you'll be measuring windows, drapes, room dimensions, carpets, light fixtures, walls, doorways, sofas, height of chests, and flatness of your wallet.

The tape measure is the second most important tool of the new homeowner. The *most* important is the checkbook.

How to Work with an Architect

Architects usually have three problems with clients (four if you count "getting paid").

First, some clients have impeccable taste and expect only the finest, but they don't want to pay more than $5 a square foot in construction costs. That's like trying to find a new Rolls-Royce on sale for $4,000.

Second, some clients can't make up their minds. No sooner has the architect completed a set of drawings than the client changes the rules of the game.

Third, still other clients believe themselves to be brilliant self-made designers. Just ask them. They have a never-ending list of suggestions, most of which destroy the integrity of the architect's design.

Give your architect a chance. When the day arrives for the initial meeting, many clients bring file folders bulging with pictures, plans, and articles clipped from various magazines. The client then instructs the architect to incorporate all these ideas exactly as featured in the magazines (usually accompanied by home-drawn plans scaled out in the wee hours of the morning).

Instead, offer your architect the freedom to create. Just describe the general features you want and ask the architect to design a house *he* likes. You'll probably be rewarded with a work of art.

Learn the lingo. Clients often have a hard time adjusting to the architect's jargon. If your architect wears a tie and uses the words *comprehensive* and *viable* repeatedly, add 15 percent to the normal fee. Just what is "viable space" anyway? I understand "cramped," "comfortable," "luxurious," and "spartan," but not "viable."

Don't ask your architect to make "blueprints" for you. That is a printing technique that has gone the way of the horse and buggy. It's rarely used for residential drawings.

"I don't want to tell you how to do your job . . .
but let me show you a few of my own ideas."

Ask the architect to "prepare a set of drawings and specs for the project." This way he'll think that you know something about the profession and may not inflate your bill too much above average.

Don't assume that architects never goof. Many past clients insist that they are living in an architect's mistake. There is a famous horse named My Mistake and a number of homes named His Mistake.

Architects sometimes draw plans that look good on paper, but not when fully executed. By the time you're finished, you may wish the architect had been executed instead of the plan. Room size and proportion are difficult to envision in full scale. Often clients fall in love with the plans but are unhappy with the finished product. It turned out too narrow, too small, too large, or too short. Yet nobody realized it just by looking at the plans.

Try to construct a rough layout of the proposed addition right in your present home. Amble over to your largest room and rope off a space equal in size to the addition. Move some furniture around to help define boundaries. You may feel a little silly running around the house with a spool of twine, tying up your furniture like some misplaced rodeo cowboy roping a stray sofa. Don't worry. It's better to be a ropin' fool for a few moments than to make a serious error. Some folks spare no effort and expense to build a room they don't like.

If you are wondering where to find a great architect, let me offer a few suggestions. The American Institute of Architects (headquartered in Washington, D.C.) represents about 25 percent of the profession, and therefore it's a good place to begin. Another suggestion is to contact the owners of homes that you particularly admire and ask for the names of the architects. There are a number of fine periodicals which feature the works of prominent architects. Especially worthwhile publications with excellent reporting are *Better Homes and Gardens, House Beautiful, House & Garden, Architectural Record,* and *Architectural Digest.* If you like the work of an architect featured in these magazines, don't hesitate to contact him directly.

Rub-α-Dub-Dub

When I was young, I watched the cowboy movies every Saturday. Day after day the cowboys rode the range, whupped the bad guys, helped the schoolmarm, and sang songs, but they never had to stop and go to the bathroom.

Now life has changed. Families spend more time in the bath each year, bathing, shaving, and putting on makeup. The only lassoing I do these days is when I plug in the hair dryer on my wife's side of our bath and wrap the cord around her in the process. Do you think Roy and Dale have these problems?

While the bad guys robbed banks and trains, we never saw the good guys work for a living. Roy, Gene, and Hopalong, riding down the street, wonder how you managed to make ends meet . . . ?

Today thousands of old fans of those Western heroes are spending unbelievable sums installing luxurious bathrooms with Jacuzzi tubs and fancy fixtures in their homes. What would Roy and Trigger think?

Like many homeowners across the country, ZsaZsa and Mort Gagor are in the midst of remodeling their bathroom. They began planning by leafing through an assortment of

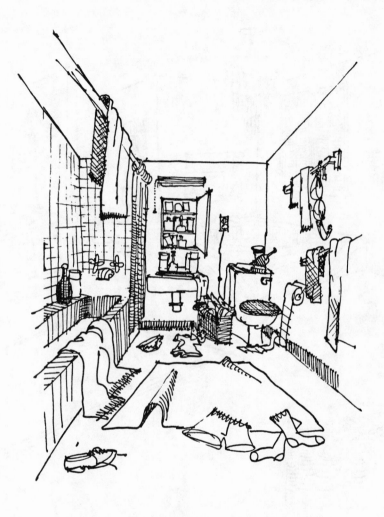

My bathroom when I was a saddle pal of Roy Rogers.

Our new bathroom now that we have
a little buckaroo of our own.

After the Saturday morning round-up . . .

books and magazines which featured photographs of elegant, sensational baths.

"Does our present bathroom resemble those fabulous photos found in the latest decorator magazines? Not in the slightest!" ZsaZsa concluded. What photograph would feature a slew of wet towels, T-shirts on the floor, an overflowing wastebasket in the center of the room, and shampoo bottles perched precariously on the edge of the bathtub? To this vision of loveliness, the Gagor family must add the three plastic fishes their son brings into the tub every day while he plays Shampoo Man. When Mort finishes shaving in the morning, ZsaZsa tells him that it looks as if a flock of ducks have made their home near the sink. Perhaps this is vaguely reminiscent of what you might find at your home.

Don't start off worrying about the choice of decoration or even fixtures, because you won't be able to see them underneath the towels, T-shirts, toothpaste tubes, and wastebaskets. Begin by developing a plan to alter the chaotic visual landscape of your soggy, sloppy, unsightly bath. As an exercise, try leafing through popular magazines looking for photos of "ideal bathrooms" with enough large and inconspicuously placed towel racks to solve the problem. This is a futile task nearly as difficult as persuading the Loch Ness Monster to appear on the "Tonight Show."

Most of the designer baths that are featured have no towel racks at all. Usually the picture shows a well-placed, elegant, fluffy towel draped seductively over the tub. At best there are several small bars or towel rings discreetly located. This does not give you a clue as to what to do with two or three massive soaking-wet bath sheets, plus an assortment of hand towels.

Photos of ideal bathrooms never show wastebaskets or piles of discarded underwear. Interior designers *do* have some real-life solutions. Bathroom vanity cabinets can be ordered with built-in fold-out wastebaskets and clothes hampers. Look around and pick the spot nearest your abandoned underclothes and locate the new built-in hamper there.

While you are at it, this is the time to plan for built-in bathroom washbasins at thirty-four or thirty-five inches above the floor instead of the usual "plumber's standard" height of thirty-one inches. The thirty-one-inch height is designed as a compromise for children and adults. It's suitable for neither. *Now's your chance to build cabinets the right height for you.* Don't let some plumber sell you a height that is "standard" but uncomfortable.

Perhaps those sloppy people who leave their bathrooms messy will not do one bit better even with built-in hampers and wastebaskets. You can lead a horse to water, but you probably can't make him put the cap back on the toothpaste tube.

Shopping for a bathtub is like trying to find a comfortable pair of shoes. It's important to get a good fit. The exact proportions of the ideal bathtub vary with your size. The rule of thumb is simple: *the tub should be the same length as the owner.* This will allow the bather to stretch out fully and relax.

Unfortunately, the standard bathtub installed in 90 percent of all homes in this country is only five feet long. The height of the average American woman is five feet five, and the height of the average man is five feet ten. You don't need Sherlock Holmes to figure out that there are many uncomfortable bathers.

Archeologists of future generations may develop misconceptions when they uncover the ruins of our baths, theorizing that twentieth-century Americans were a pygmy race whose height rarely exceeded five feet.

There are numerous factors to consider when designing the perfect bathtub: the slope of the ends, the height of the sides, length, placement of faucets, velocity of water, volume of the tub, contour, surface characteristics, width, cost, shape, size of bathers, number of bathers, and so forth. If you are ever in doubt about what to do, remember this easy formula to handle all of these variables:

$$\frac{\frac{\sqrt{h}}{160.2N^3}\, W\frac{18}{25}\, \nabla\, \frac{Slope^N}{12\,\#}}{(\,b^3+\sqrt{Mc^2}\,\frac{Velocity}{Temperature^2}\times 1.6\times 10^{-19})} +$$

$$\frac{\sum}{h}\frac{P\ell^3}{\delta}\int \sin\left(\frac{w\pi \ell}{4}\right) - \frac{\sqrt[3]{k^4}}{7^L}$$

If this is a bit much for you to handle, then just keep in mind when designing your tub the immortal words of Duke Ellington, "It don't mean a thing if it ain't got that swing." Wing it if you must.

All this is reminiscent of Goldilocks and the three bears. You are looking for a tub that is not too big, not too small, not too hot, not too cold, but just right! Most tubs have

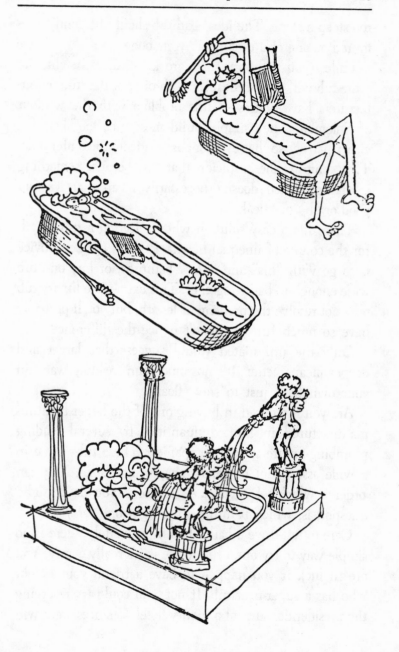

too steep a slope. The ideal bathtub should be gently contoured at one end to support your body.

Unless you and your mate are identical in height, the same tub will not be ideal for both of you. Bathtub manufacturers have addressed this problem with the wisdom of Solomon. They simply build most tubs too short for either partner so that everyone is relatively uncomfortable. This confirms the suspicion that just because something is mass-produced doesn't necessarily mean that it's (a) good or (b) practical.

There is no easy solution when selecting a tub length for the couple of unequal height. Perhaps the best advice is to go with "his" and "hers" bathtubs, or buy one tub wide enough to bathe together. This extra-wide luxury tub may not resolve the problem of length, but you'll probably have so much fun you won't notice the difference.

Only the uninitiated would suggest that larger and deeper means better. It's not much fun treading water in your own bath just to stay afloat.

Are you interested in buying one of the larger bathtubs manufactured in limited quantities by several leading plumbing-fixture supply companies? These tubs come in a wide assortment of colors, shapes, and sizes. You can order a whirlpool or Jacuzzi feature if you desire. The question is, which bathtub is the right one for you?

Care to test-drive a bathtub? Unfortunately, there is no simple way to try out a tub to see if it's really comfy. You are in luck if you happen to have a friend your height who has a super-neat tub. If not, you could try reserving the presidential suite at a luxury hotel. Chances are it will come equipped with a custom-designed large tub. But the cost of traveling the country to test tubs in suites might exceed the price you were hoping to pay for remodeling your entire bathroom.

The practical solution is to visit plumbing fixture showrooms. Crawl into their tubs when no one is looking. After several days of climbing into bathtubs in showrooms (twice we were discovered by salesmen who did their best to hide their amusement), Suzanne and I concluded that some savvy plumbing supplier should set up a showroom complete with running water and test tubs. This idea may not have real commercial feasibility. There was *not* a long line of people standing ahead of us in the showrooms, waiting to jump into the tubs.

> Rub-a-dub-dub,
> Three men in a tub;
> And who do you think they be?
> If the salesmen are not watching,
> My wife, my son, and me.

The Family Room
and the Family of Man

In many countries, families are forced to live crowded together in one room. They dream of owning large, beautifully furnished homes with numerous rooms. Here in America, this dream can become a reality. Yet many who own spacious homes choose to live together in one scarred, battered, and worn room—the family room. If you don't have a room like this already, chances are you want to build one. The rest of the house can often be found covered in plastic and reserved for "company." And even when "company" comes, they are usually ushered into the family room.

Homo sapiens is a gregarious species given to frolicking in a small, casually furnished area. This family area should be near the kitchen so that the entire family can cavort back and forth regularly to the refrigerator. It should be located close to the bathroom for quick trips during commercials.

Perhaps a course in zoological architecture should be a basic requirement for all residential designers. A well-run zoo would use the following checklist of requirements for building animal enclosures:

1. *An adequate amount of space.* Tolstoy may have decided in his story "How Much Space Does a Man Need" that ultimately it is six feet by two, but we know better. You need space to spread out your Scrabble board, Erector set, and dollhouse furniture just as much as the fur seal at the zoo needs a fair-sized pool to splash about in.

2. *Freedom from boredom.* Cabin fever can strike at any time, just as easily for you as for the polar bear in his sunken box with visitors' rail. Your cage needs something you can sit and stare at too. Usually it's a television set.

3. *A place for the inhabitants to get away from each other.* Let's face it, there will be days when you are at each other's throats. It happens to the best of us.

4. *Efficient access for cleaning enclosures.* The zoo-

keeper and the homeowner have a lot in common. Neither wants to get a backache crawling around under shelves and ledges carefully retrieving yesterday's droppings. Hotel maids have the cleaning game down to a fine art. They can straighten a bed or tidy a bathroom in seconds flat. Zookeepers and homeowners tend to be fussier.

5. *A nook for storing food and water.* We call it the refrigerator. Enough said.

The chest-beating *Homo sapiens* is likely to prepare a similar list for his architect. Zoo directors must reconcile the goal of providing good public display with the objective of comfortable enclosures for the animals. The average homeowner is confronted with the same trade-off.

Modern man clings to the family room. If you don't believe that we are still primitive mammals, then why do you think we call it a den?

Doing the Backstroke
and the Backwash

Have you decided to forgo the long trek to the beach this year and build a swimming pool in your backyard instead? Why risk long lines at the gas pumps when you can conserve energy and have fun at home? We might also help solve our energy crisis if we could get some of the oil off of the beaches and into the refineries. Environmentalists warn that the lakes and streams we used to enjoy are so polluted that even the fish have put up signs saying "Off Limits."

Americans are an ingenious people, quick with alternatives. Many have responded to the recreational as well as the environmental crisis by building a swimming pool at home. Hearty American individualists have rejected both car pools and community swimming pools.

The process of building your own pool is easy. All you'll need is a gigantic earth mover, seventy tons of concrete, coping materials, lights, filter pit, chlorinator, skimmers, pump, and 37,000 gallons of city-owned water. You may also have to call a landscape service to try to remove the concrete truck's tire marks from the lawn.

Once the pool has been installed, you will immediately notice that the backyard just disappeared. Grass, flowers, and trees are only fond memories. Of course you can still tell the season of the year by the changes in water temperature.

Your pool can bring many hours of pleasure (for your neighbors) after *you* have: checked the strainers for leaves, skimmed off the bugs, performed sophisticated chemical analysis of the water, dumped in soda ash, backwashed the pool, and cleaned the patio. Swimming pools do provide good exercise, but not necessarily the type you expect.

Let's Put the "Kitsch" Back in Kitchen

It's time to remodel your kitchen when you suddenly discover that all your appliances are older than you are. One day my wife Suzanne announced that she *had* to redo our kitchen.

"Imagine!" she said. "We could save a *lot* of money stocking up on sale-priced specials if we had tons of storage space. Give me enough counter space and dinner will change from cheeseburgers with Hamburger Helper to a dazzling array of haute cuisine gourmet delights. Let's build a big country kitchen that will be the hub of the household, the key to family togetherness. With a fantastic kitchen, who needs vacation trips to the Caribbean or even new clothes?"

"It's yours," I said helplessly.

To build yourself the latest in modern family kitchens, just follow this utterly foolproof Cordon Bleu recipe for remodeling your present run-of-the-mill beanery.

The stark metal and white-paint look of the fifties is definitely out. Pink tiles and bleached wood cabinets are as passé as Doris Day and Rock Hudson movies. Gone too are the sterile moonshot hygiene of the sixties and the French chef, sanitary steel look of the seventies. The kitchen of the eighties is as much "kitsch" as "in."

Modern homeowners want a fun kitchen. Anyone can efficiently microwave up a frozen gourmet dinner, but it's much more fun to get the whole family together to create a real old-fashioned country lentil soup. The country kitchen, with its roomy atmosphere and bustling togetherness, is the tradition of tomorrow.

The rustic look is in. Buy some real wood cabinets, butcher-block countertops, and cane chairs. Don't sacrifice convenience, though. You'll need a built-in microwave oven above your self-cleaning regular oven (the latter for home-baked bread, of course). Don't worry if you can't manage a picture window over the kitchen sink with a view of the kids' play area and your victory garden. Just hang up a Currier and Ives print of a covered bridge and imagine the horses' hooves clattering across as you load your new dishwasher with rinse, dry, and potscrubber cycles.

You'll need a breakfast nook, naturally. Why not buy a good solid oak round table where you can all chat over a friendly game of checkers?

In this age of energy conservation, your family's activities will naturally gravitate toward the warmth of the kitchen. Some families are even installing Swedish energy-saving wood stoves.

Today's ideal kitchen is, in short, a country retreat within an urbane home. Go ahead and give it the works. Use fabrics in warm earth tones; put in copper kettles and real solid oak beams. Hang up some dried vegetables any Spanish-onion seller would be proud to sling over his shoulder. Try drying your own herbs in bunches over the cellar door. As a final touch, consider the picturesque effect of a collection of antique bottles, preferably leather and slightly dusty.

Then stand back and proudly take a good look at what you've created: your very own turn-of-the-century log-cabin kitchen with all the modern conveniences.

Scarlett and Rhett

Most men who have seen *Gone with the Wind* secretly desire to play the role of Captain Rhett Butler. His virile power, good looks, and ill-gotten riches seduced Scarlett into a tumultuous marriage. After their honeymoon fling among the adventurers and scoundrels of New Orleans, Scarlett and Rhett returned to Atlanta. The first thing they did was build a new house: a garish, lavish, expensively furnished mansion designed to make the respectable but impoverished Atlanta "Old Guard" society pea-green with envy.

In the novel and film version of *Gone with the Wind*, the marriage between Rhett and Scarlett goes on the rocks because of Scarlett's indestructible love for Ashley Wilkes.

In a "real life" version of *Gone with the Wind*, it is doubtful that the marriage of these two strong-willed individuals would have survived the building and furnishing of their Atlanta house. The first time Scarlett announced, "Oh, Rhett, there are not enough closets, and we must have our new red wallpaper replaced with something tangerine," it's likely Rhett would have walked out the door and said, "Frankly, my dear, I don't give a damn."

Mad King Ludwig

Meet Mad King Ludwig, builder of fairyland palaces and pillager of Bavaria's treasury. If castle building be the sport of kings, Ludwig is the reigning champion. Enraptured with his castles, he went on a building spree that ended in 1886 and nearly bankrupted the kingdom.

Disdaining the affairs of state, he made ministers wait for weeks on end while he pursued castle building and furnishing. Emulating King Louis XIV of France, he built his Herrenchiemsee Palace after the model of Versailles. By his order a reproduction of the famed Hall of Mirrors was created, even larger and more luxurious than the original.

The artistic appetite of the King demanded more and more gorgeous furnishings. Artisans worked for seven years on the curtains of his bedroom alone. (You think *you* have to wait a long time for deliveries.) Louis XIV's bedroom pales before King Ludwig's unbelievably ornate golden boudoir complete with Meissen mirrors, semi-precious stones, and crystal chandeliers.

Not content with the castles he built at Neuschwanstein, Linderhof, and Herrenchiemsee, Ludwig talked of building a fourth castle even more expensive and grandiose than his others.

In despair, Ludwig's ministers plotted to have him certified insane. An eccentric living in a dream world, he was deposed in 1886 and died a few days later at the age of forty-one.

King Ludwig was by no means the only one to get carried away while building a dream house. Although his state castles are imposing, it is not necessary to travel to Herrenchiemsee (first go to Neuschwanstein, then take a right) in order to find other examples.

The largest privately owned house in the world is the 250-room Biltmore House in Asheville, North Carolina. Can you imagine *furnishing* 250 rooms? The house was built on an estate of 119,000 acres. The house and land cost $4 million when it was constructed by a Vanderbilt in the 1890s. Today the house and 112 acres of the surrounding land are valued at $60 million.

The most costly private house ever built belonged to William Randolph Hearst and is located at San Simeon, California. It was built during 1922–1939 at a cost of more than $30 million. The house has more than 100 rooms, a garage for twenty-five limousines, and a 104-foot-long heated swimming pool. Hearst required a mere sixty servants to maintain it.

Some private folks go in for regal pleasures! Misery loves company. Relax, you're not alone. What's an extra $10,000 or $20,000 compared to the follies of Ludwig?

And They Lived
Happily Ever After

Moving Day

The Pilgrims crossed the Atlantic in the *Mayflower*. That tiny vessel carried 102 passengers with all their possessions, together with twenty-five crew members and enough food and water for the long voyage. The main hold of the ship was approximately eighty feet long, ten feet deep, and twenty-two feet in width. That's about 17,000 cubic feet. No one knows for certain how much space was devoted to the ship's stores as opposed to family possessions. It's likely that each person on board had approximately 100 cubic feet of storage space.

The American Movers Conference reports that the average American family requires approximately one-third of a moving van to transport their household goods. That is, they need about 800 cubic feet for a family of four, or 200 cubic feet per person.

In our case, Suzanne, our young son, and I required 90 percent of a moving van, or approximately 2,100 cubic feet. That's 700 cubic feet per person, or seven times the space any Pilgrim was allowed, and we didn't have to carry grain, axes, or building supplies.

Only one-third of our van was filled with furniture. We're about average in that department. Two-thirds of the van was filled with a phenomenal amount of "stuff":

records, books, papers, plants, clothes we don't wear anymore, toys, more toys, and junk. We've come a long way
since the Pilgrim days, but I'm not sure you'd call it
progress.

Moving is a good time to become philosophical and
question the value of the pursuit and collection of material
possessions. Do you really need all this stuff? Will *more*
bring you happiness?

Most of us wear 20 percent of our wardrobe 90 percent
of the time. Why keep carting around the other 80 percent? Even if the styles come back into fashion, the clothes
probably won't fit.

Moving day also provides a fine illustration of the
scientific principle of inertia. An object at rest tends to stay
at rest. After the move, it takes a great deal of courage to
start sorting out the boxes. One family told us they had
almost all their boxes put away only a year and a half after
the move.

In the Old Testament story of the flight from Egypt,
the Israelites had to pack up and leave overnight. Some
say that they made unleavened bread in the desert because
they had to leave Egypt so quickly that there wasn't time
to let the bread dough rise. Now I realize that story is not
totally accurate. More likely than not, they just couldn't
remember in which box they packed the yeast.

Tax-Saving Tips

The tax laws are complicated, but there are many tax
breaks available to homeowners. Homeownership entitles

you to a number of tax deductions that can save you money.

Mortgage Interest and Real-Estate Taxes

The two major deductions of benefit to all homeowners who itemize their tax deductions are the amounts paid for mortgage loan interest and real-estate taxes.

The good news is that mortgage loan interest and real-estate taxes are deductible. The bad news is that property taxes and interest rates are so unbelievably high that you'll have *big* deductions.

Depreciation and Home Improvements

Homeowners are *not* allowed to take a depreciation expense on their residence. However, you can deduct the costs of the improvements you make to your house at the time you *sell* it.

Keep a record of the costs of all the improvements made to your home. Improvements might include room additions, landscaping, fences, swimming pools, patios, storm windows, and air conditioners. The cost of all these improvements can be added to the original purchase price of your house in order to reduce the amount of gain on the sale. It's necessary to have detailed records to substantiate these costs. Keep a file at home for all your home-improvement bills.

Tax Credits for Energy Conservation

In 1978 Congress passed a bill that entitles homeowners to certain tax credits if they undertake a home-improvement program to conserve energy. This credit applies to various energy-saving improvements, including exterior caulking, weatherstripping, storm doors and windows, and insulation.

These tax credits cover only items installed between May 1977 and December 1985. The law applies only to existing homes that were substantially built before May 1977. You can contact the Treasury Department for additional information.

This new energy program permits homeowners to take 15 percent of the first $2,000 spent on certain energy-saving home improvements as a tax credit—up to a maximum of $300.

The problem is that in today's world of skyrocketing inflation, by the time most of us buy a house, make the mortgage payments, and pay the utility bills, we're so broke that we don't have the $2,000 to spend in order to get the $300 tax credit. Now if only Uncle Sam would loan us the $2,000 to spend in the first place. . . .

Homeowners who install geothermal, wind, or solar energy-saving devices are entitled to a tax credit of 30 percent on the first $2,000 spent, plus 20 percent of the next $8,000, for a maximum tax credit of $2,200.

This credit differs from the previously mentioned home-improvement credit in that it applies to homes built either before or after May 1977. But, as they say, it takes money to make money.

Tax-Free Exchange—Deferred Taxes When You Sell

If you sell and make a profit, the profit is taxable in the current year. If, however, you reinvest in another residence that costs at least as much as your last home within eighteen months of the date you sold that home, the taxes on the profit are deferred indefinitely.

I used to wonder why the IRS wanted to use tax policy to motivate homeowners to buy another house within eighteen months of the sale. Now I think I've come up with the answer. If people sell their homes for a profit and move into apartments, the IRS is probably concerned that they'll live it up and spend their loot. Without the burden and expense of a big home, the footloose fancy-free apartment dwellers will probably start going out to expensive restaurants, buying new clothes, traveling abroad, and blowing their housing profits on a good time The government wisely figures it had better collect the tax from these folks right away while they've still got it.

Most homeowners have no problem complying with the provision of the tax law requiring them to purchase another home at least as expensive as their old one in order to qualify for a fully deferred tax on reinvestment. After a few weeks of looking, homeowners soon discover that they couldn't possibly buy *any* new home as cheaply as they sold their old one!

U.S. government policy is concerned with motivating homeowners to keep on buying homes. It's a wise move for incumbent politicians to maintain this policy. Governments tend to remain stable in countries with many suburban single-family homeowners. The poor homeowner is so exhausted from commuting, working to make mortgage payments, cutting the grass, and repairing broken appliances that he barely takes time to vote, let alone change the political system or start a revolution.

Carefree apartment dwellers in big cities have the time and money to start uprisings. If Karl Marx had had a home in suburbia with two cars that were constantly breaking down, he'd have been too busy to have started the Communist party. The only party most homeowners join is the Tupperware party. As Mrs. Marx sadly remarked upon her husband's death, "If only Karl hadn't talked so much about capital and had made more of it. . . ."

Once-in-a-Lifetime $100,000 Tax Break

The 1978 tax law gives homeowners who are fifty-five years old or more a tax-free profit of up to $100,000 on the sale of their principal residence.

The homeowner must have owned and occupied the home for three of the last five years in order to qualify. If you are nearing age fifty-five, you should wait until you reach your fifty-fifth birthday before selling your home. It is not necessary to reinvest the profits in another home to obtain this tax break.

Clearly, this provision of the tax law was designed to let older homeowners sell their large homes and move into apartments or smaller homes without paying any tax penalty. In its infinite wisdom, Congress decided that it would not cause undue political unrest to have citizens over age fifty-five become apartment dwellers. Let's face it, not many revolutions are started by people who have just made a $100,000 profit on the sale of their home.

Good Karma

Many people believe that entering the exalted state of homeownership will endow them with mystical powers, creative surges, peace of mind, sexual attractiveness, and instant glory. They are not searching for bricks and mortar, but an improved mental condition.

Instead of finding a Maharishi to teach you a secret Indian mantra for meditation, try closing your eyes, sitting still, and chanting the word *home* to yourself for about thirty minutes a day. It sounds a lot like *om*, the Maharishi's chosen word. This chanting may produce a state of higher consciousness and lower blood pressure. Then again, it may not.

On the beach last summer I noticed a pretty woman wearing a T-shirt that proclaimed, "I've stopped looking for the truth. I'd settle for a good fantasy." House fever can bring on a serious case of wishful thinking. There's nothing wrong with a good healthy fantasy or two.

My friend Gerald is an example of the romantic type looking for a magical mansion. One day he came over and announced, "If I owned a really impressive home, the girls would fall in love with me. A never-ending stream of girls . . . fashion models, cheerleaders, southern belles, and budding starlets would come to my home.

"First I need to find a spectacular dream house set in lush landscaped grounds, with a bubbly Jacuzzi bath, candlelit dining room, bedroom with mirrored ceilings, and a free-form swimming pool. Once I have a fine home, beautiful young girls will come to play. Girls in bikinis will meet at my pool."

"Do you really think that a house will solve all your problems and light up your love life?" I asked. "Have you considered just trying a new toothpaste or mouthwash? It's a lot cheaper."

"No, I must have the house," Gerald said adamantly. "I can picture it now. . . ."

"So, this is your home!" the girl said.

"Make yourself comfortable," Gerald reassured her.

The girl stood in the center of the room and admired everything in sight. "Here's your drink," said Gerald.

"Thank you," she whispered.

"Come sit down," he said, leading her to the heavily cushioned velvet sofa.

"It's warmer than leather," he said quietly. She snuggled against him, looking eager and innocent.

I slipped out quietly, not wanting to disturb Gerald's daydreams. He was so enraptured with the visions of ecstasy in his new dream home-to-be that he never even noticed me leaving.

Your fantasy may run along the lines of Edgar and Gertrude, the New Pioneers.

"Now that our children have grown up and left us, it's time for a second honeymoon. We don't need this big house to rattle around in. Let's buy a motor home and see the country, Gertrude," Edgar said enthusiastically to his bride of the past thirty-some years. "Think of the freedom and fun of traveling the open road."

"But Edgar," Gertrude protested, "the children still need us here. They're counting on our help with the grand-children. And think of our friends. We'd miss a lot if we sold our home."

"Why, that motor home I've got my eye on would be more fun than a dozen Volkswagens. It's just about the handiest vehicle around. It can carry us into mountains and campsites. We'll make a new life with new friends after we sell this old house."

Gertrude sighed as she thought of the trials of keeping a clean household while traveling through the country and how much she would miss the grandchildren. "Still," she thought, "Edgar may be right. Why just sit around and grow old?"

"Come on, Gert," said Edgar. "For a couple of old timers, we'll feel good truckin' on down the road."

"But what will our children think?" said Gertrude.

"Why, we're old enough to do what we want. Our youngsters care too much for drab clothes and drab con-ventions for my taste," snorted Edgar. "This is our chance to live a little. It's about time. We can come and go as we please, move around as we like. Plenty of retired people over sixty are on the road. Let's get some Lawrence Welk tapes, sell the house, and GO."

Ode to the Road

Just because I'm sixty-four
Shall I not travel anymore?
Must I stay home and mow the grass
Or should I sell, and move out fast?

Let's not live our days
From end to middle
Watching TV
And getting brittle.

What better time
To romp and roam
Behind the wheel
Of a motor home.

One of my acquaintances who made his dreams come true was Joseph. I met him by chance in a local bistro.

The tall, thin young man who entered the coffee shop had western-style jeans and shoulder-length hair. He was almost twenty-six and wore a faded blue shirt, tooled leather belt, and Earth shoes. He grinned a lot and bobbed in place, as though he were listening to the radio.

"And you," I said, shaking hands, "must be Joseph. I've been looking forward to meeting you. So you're the fellow who single-handedly built a handcrafted house."

He nodded, grinned, and bobbed. "Really, building a house yourself is a celebration of the mind, body, and spirit," said Joseph.

"Could you show me what your house is like?" I asked.

He opened a canvas knapsack and took out some photographs.

"It's natural, cheap, and has a lot of me in it," he said. "Not some ticky-tacky box that enslaves us to the mentality of the middle-class establishment. My house is hand hewn. It's built with genuine love and carefully selected wood. Building your own home unites the rift between outer and inner man."

"You don't say," I said. "I can see your house-building experience has deeply influenced your outlook on life."

"Good karma," agreed Joseph. "For me, building my home merges my work with my identity."

Joseph was fully conscious of what his house meant to him. It wasn't just a shelter to keep out the elements. It was part of him.

"It's really getting my space and time into the same plane," he explained.

Your house projects a style, an identity. Don't forget that you have an identity apart from the house. You own it. It does not own you (although some days that's hard to believe). It's easy to lose track of where your identity stops and the house begins.

Inferior Decorator versus Interior Decorator

When Blanche and Reuben Garnish came across a bucolic retreat, they knew at once it was the house they wanted. Their hillside home is everything you would expect a successful pickle-packer prince's home to be.

The Garnishes are direct descendants of Rachel and Myron Garnishinski. These itinerant peasants were lucky to own a table and chair in the old country. Rachel and Myron didn't collect fine period furniture. They were mainly into flight and survival.

Blanche and Reuben quickly realized that good design is the expression of imposing their will upon amorphousness in a persuasive spirit of clarity. Moreover, it costs big bucks!

On August 22, the Garnishes stopped at the office of well-known interior designer, Jarrett Smyth. The receptionist said that none of the staff professionals were available. It would be necessary to wait several weeks for an appointment. In the meantime, the Garnishes decided to visit several other decorators, only to discover that they too were either busy or out. Blanche and Reuben encountered an unwritten rule among some quality designers: *Make the client wait.*

By the time a client finally gets to see the interior designers, weeks have passed, and the client considers it a privilege to have a few moments of their time.

On September 8, the time finally arrived for the meeting with Jarrett. He arranged for the visit to take place at the Garnish home, so that they could discuss the project on-site.

Jarrett arrived promptly and proceeded to tell the Garnishes what a wonderful house they had chosen. As they toured from room to room, he started off by asking Blanche what she had in mind. Soon the three were discussing changes in the carpeting, wallpaper, drapes, and paint. Smyth knowingly referred to this part of the process as "preparing the shell." The Garnishes learned what he meant by "the shell." The walls, floors, ceilings, and windows are the shell for the furnishings to come.

After they had spent a fortune for their magnificent new home, it was a little demoralizing to hear it called a shell. And what's worse, it actually was a shell that needed to be completely redecorated. At this point Blanche and Reuben began to wonder why they had just paid so much for a house whose charm was rapidly fading under the designer's critical eye.

Jarrett then suggested that he take the time to design a floor plan for furnishings. He volunteered to select colors, fabric swatches, and carpet samples to make a complete presentation for refurbishing the house. Jarrett praised the quintessential spirit of the house and intimated that he had many ideas for honest and timeless quality decoration. The Garnishes were impressed. Another meeting was arranged several weeks later for Jarrett's presentation. They were once again in a holding pattern, still circling, while living in an almost empty house.

By September 20, nearly a month had transpired since the initial visit to the designer's office. Blanche and Reuben were finally to learn how the decorator would approach their house. A second unwritten rule of many successful decorators is: *Sell them a room at a time.* Instead of acting like the average furniture salesman who asks if you might be interested in a lamp or a chair, a good interior designer looks at the big picture and offers a proposal for an entire room.

Smyth showed them fabric swatches, paint chips, carpet samples, and sketches of furniture arrangements. These sales aids were quite helpful. His work allowed them to visualize completed rooms clearly.

Once Blanche and Reuben started nodding their approval, Jarrett knew that his sale was almost made. They might want to change one or two pieces of furniture, but the Garnishes realized that if too many good pieces were taken out of the rooms that Jarrett presented, the total feeling would be lost. By focusing on the room as the product, most people agree that deleting more than a few items destroys the vision.

Blanche and Reuben initially thought of going to their decorator for a few suggestions on carpet texture or wall color, perhaps just to pick up an occasional lamp or chair. The designer had other plans.

Be prepared. It is hard to resist temptation and the interior decorator does a great job of playing the devil. Deep down you know you have already spent too much for your house. Save some money for a rainy day. Adam couldn't resist the apple and few latter-day Adams or Eves can withstand the temptation of a magnificently furnished room to accompany their new house. The lesson is: *Don't take the first bite of the apple, because it is hard to resist the second.* You have started down the path the minute you let the interior designer prepare a formal presentation. If you have chosen poorly and selected an inferior decorator, you are just wasting your time. But if you selected a fine artist, you are heading down the path of want and ruin as your bank account begins to dwindle.

If all you really wanted in the first place was a little advice on what color to paint your new living room, then say so. Make it quite clear from the start that you don't intend to spend much money and might be willing to buy a few small pieces in return for some advice.

It is more fun to intimate that you have scads of money and are only awaiting the suggestions of the decorator in order to spend it. You might start out thinking you will fool the decorator into giving you some free advice if he thinks you are a real pigeon for a big order. Most clients only fool themselves and end up by giving the interior designer that very big order.

Blanche and Reuben Garnish were no exception, although they managed to come away relatively unscathed. They spent a mere $20,000 with their interior decorator. They would have spent more, but that was all the money they had.

Caveat Emptor

Trying to furnish a house can be extremely exasperating. The three biggest lies in the English language are: "The check is in the mail"; "My wife doesn't understand me"; "Delivery will be in eight to ten weeks."

If you thought the hunt and the catch were bad, the keep and the upkeep are worse. Next to buying a house, decorating it may be the biggest investment of your life. This may sound preposterous, but for many it's true.

Some of us are very fortunate to have inherited all the right pieces from dear old Aunt Martha. Others only inherited Aunt Primrose's lovely cameos or Uncle Larry's bottle-cap collection. For the latter legacy, a trip to the furniture store is a must.

Before buying a home, the Braunstein family motto was *If you can't sit on it, lie on it, or eat on it, then you don't need it!* Up until the day we bought our house, we managed nicely with a minimum of furniture.

I don't want to suggest that Suzanne and I didn't have much furniture, but when our new neighbors came to visit after we moved in, they said, "Well, when are you going to make the big move?"

"We already did," I gulped. "After all, it's a large house and we just spread the furniture around a bit." We all stood staring into a large empty formal living room.

Nature's creatures are born with an innate urge to put personal markings on their abodes. This hasn't changed in the past few hundred thousand years. Like the cavemen of yesteryear, modern *Homo sapiens americanus* still can't resist the desire to monkey around and redecorate.

I wish I had a nickel for every time that a relative or friend has uttered to us those immortal words, "Don't change anything. First, live in the house for a while. Try it, you'll like it."

We tried that, and what had initially been considered a tormented wallpaper design grew less objectionable. However, the ghastly murky shag wall-to-wall carpet that seemed to devour anything that was dropped on it still remained the ghastly murky shag.

The second case clearly shows that your first instinct is right. If you don't like it, remove it. The first case, in which you've become reconciled with the object, does not necessarily prove that your initial instinct was wrong. It may be that (a) you're just too cheap to change it; (b) you have actually grown to like it (tsk tsk); or (c) you don't give a damn anymore.

There is no use worrying too much about what type of furniture to select. By the time you have bought the house, there won't be any money left for furniture. The few dollars that you can scrape together must be carefully allocated.

Should you buy quality or quantity? You need a houseful of furniture. If you buy inexpensive pieces there's a chance of filling up the house. But you could buy just a few good pieces and continue to live in an almost empty home. It seems wiser to go for quality, but it looks darn silly for the whole family to be standing around an empty room looking at one good chair.

When you first move in, the major concern is getting the house ready to show friends and family. Don't worry and don't wait until your decorating is complete. That may take years. My Aunt Sadie took me aside one day and pointed out that "your home will *never* be ready. There is always something to do."

Give a party right away and invite all your friends, neighbors, and relatives over to the empty new house. It will be obvious that you have just moved in and no one expects you to have the house together.

I told my wife that if anyone asks why our house is empty, just tell them we're so nouveau riche the furniture hasn't arrived yet. We "arrived" before it did.

When we finally got around to looking for the right pieces, we found out that what you see is not what you get. Shopping for furniture should be fun. It should be, but it isn't. The problem is that the stores usually won't sell you their best pieces off the floor. Those are often floor samples. Instead, you have to place an order and wait and wait for delivery.

Often the only furniture they'll let you have immediately are the items that have gone out of style, the buyer's mistakes. The salespeople usually offer you these by saying, "We might be able to release that piece from the floor. Let me see if I can get permission."

"Release" it? They'd be lucky to sell it if it were marked down 80 percent. When you hear that line, watch out! For you only, they *may* be able to release it. This illustrates *Braunstein's First Law of Decorating: If they'll sell it to you, you don't want it.*

"Don't worry," says the furniture salesperson. "We can have it for you in eight to ten weeks." Hah! If you believe that, could I interest you in the Brooklyn Bridge?

When you decide to order some furniture, the store may ask for a deposit to secure the order (and to use your money to finance their purchases from the factory). If months drag on past the promised delivery date, and your furniture is still not in sight, you might decide to stop aggravating yourself and cancel the order. That could be only the beginning of your problems. Try getting the deposit back.

Before you give a deposit, require the store to give you a letter agreeing to return your deposit if the merchandise doesn't arrive by the delivery date initially quoted.

This is called putting your money where your mouth is.

Now you're about to discover the *real* delivery date. The store management will probably start to squirm and wiggle away from the originally promised date. They may say that they can never be certain of the exact date, all kinds of things can happen (and they usually do), and the manufacturer will not agree to refunds of their deposits. In all likelihood, the furniture store will ask for four to eight months before agreeing to refund your deposit. This is probably closer to the true delivery date.

If you cannot get the store to agree in writing to refund your deposit by a specific date and you still go ahead with the order (boy, have you got it bad), then at least be mentally prepared to kiss the deposit good-bye or wait two years for the furniture, whichever comes first.

As long as you can get your deposit back without a hassle, don't worry if the furniture you ordered never comes. It's easy to find something else. Which brings me to *Braunstein's Second Law of Decorating: Once you order a piece of furniture, you'll find something similar you like better that costs less.*

The problem is the store won't sell you *that* piece either. You can place your order and start waiting all over again.

Swiss Francs, Iowa Pork Bellies, and Austrian Curtains

If you are looking for a sure thing with better than average potential for capital appreciation, I'd advise you to go "long" on curtains. The initial investment seems incredible, but the upside potential is substantial. You might seek out an investment adviser with a winning track record, follow the astrology column, or speculate on the latest hot tip that you heard at the office (Dallas in the Super Bowl by seven points)—none of these approaches is likely to equal the returns from your dangling damasks.

Custom-made, piped, bordered, and double-lined curtains can cost as much as the down payment for a house. A good chintz fabric ordered from a fashionable decorator costs up to $45 per yard. (At those prices, they should stop calling it chintz!) An exotic batik or printed taffeta can run up to $100 per yard. Heaven only knows what real gold lamé or brocade would cost. Ever consider a new Singer and a trip to the local fabric barn?

Classy curtains are so outrageously expensive that it's practically as economical to sew together dollar bills and drape the money over your windows. It may look a little tacky, but it's worth considering.

I calculated that if you took one-dollar bills and sewed them together to make curtain fabric, it would require approximately 120 dollar bills to make one yard of fabric with a standard fifty-four-inch width. Money, by the way, has a two-inch repeat in the pattern. Not bad, when you consider some large prints have a thirty- to forty-inch repeat.

The use of dollar bills for decorator fabric opens up new possibilities when you run short of cash. Just turn your long formal curtains into café curtains. Take the scraps and spend them.

When you tire of the design (the green may clash with your new aqua love seat), just unravel the curtains and cash in the loose bills. If you are redecorating using an Oriental motif, stop at a currency exchange and trade the

U.S. greenbacks for colorful Japanese yen. Why not try francs with French Provincial or pounds with English Regency? If all else fails, take the money and purchase some fabric. With the present high rate of inflation and the weakness of the dollar, you would be better off investing in the fabric than holding onto the money.

When you cash in your $120-a-yard dollar-bill curtains ten years from now, the money may not even buy a good chintz. You might be better off investing in a fancy taffeta now and staying with it. One well-known brokerage firm recently put out a "buy" recommendation on flocked velvet and reported that curtains closed today up 1⅜.

George Washington Slept Here

The other night Suzanne and I were at a neighborhood block party when one woman whispered to us over her second helping of potato salad, *"You know, your house will not really be yours until you sell it."*

There is a lot to be said for this observation. She had been living in the neighborhood for over five years, yet people still referred to her house as "The Old Rutherford Place." No doubt when the Rutherfords lived there, the house was probably called "The Old Jones House" after its original owners.

As newcomers to a neighborhood, you should be aware that in the years to come your neighbors will think of you as living in somebody else's home, like "The Old Ruther-

ford Place." Through all the years you live in the neighborhood, you may never have the satisfaction of having
your house known as your own. But the day it's sold, the
home you have lived in for so many years will suddenly
be known as yours, now that it belongs to someone else.

Epilogue

Everybody is hunting for something. Parents with toddlers are looking for swing sets. Swinging single junior executives are hunting for a condominium with sex appeal. Wives of recently transferred middle-aged executives are searching for a five-bedroom split-level in a good school district. Senior executives with graying temples are looking for a young mistress with a secluded flat.

Newlyweds are feathering their nests. Empty nesters are moving to the Sunbelt. College students are packing their gear for the Snowbelts. Recent college graduates are looking for the "in" apartment community.

Men in ties are looking for an inflation hedge with trees. Men in Lincoln Continentals are hunting for an "executive special." Young couples with no money are looking for a "handyman's special." Movie stars are looking for something special in the Canyon or Beverly Hills at a million dollars plus.

Restless city folks are looking for a place in the country. Young people raised on farms are hunting for a place in the city. Women with green thumbs and Gucci loafers are hunting for greenhouses.

Everybody is hunting for something. Once in a while, somebody finds it.